A PRIVATE HOUSE OF PRAYER

Leslie D. Weatherhead

Abingdon Nashville

A PRIVATE HOUSE OF PRAYER
A Festival Book

Copyright © 1958 by Leslie D. Weatherhead
Abingdon Festival edition February 1979

ISBN 0-687-34220-1
Printed in the U.S.A.

In order to offer this edition to the reader at the lowest possible price and to bring some references up to date, deletion and revision of text has been carried out where necessary.

It is hoped that no copyright has been infringed by the use of any quoted material. Apology is made and pardon asked if there be any instance to the contrary. Where authorship could not be traced, the letters S.U. (Source Unknown) are given. Prayers not referenced are Dr. Weatherhead's own. Special acknowledgments are made to the following:

ACKNOWLEDGMENTS

Appleton-Century-Crofts, Inc., for "To a Waterfowl," from *Collected Poems* by William Cullen Bryant.

B. McCall Barbour for "The Weary One Had Rest"

Dr. Alexander Bell and the proprietors of *The Woman's Magazine* for "To Each His Vision," by Doris Holden.

The Bishop of Sheffield for the hymn "Dear Master, in Whose Life I See" by his father, John Hunter.

The Rev. Wilfrid H. Bourne for his comment on Hebrews and quotation on p. 183.

Mr. Alfred W. Braithwaite for "O might I scape the sordid city air."

The *British Medical Journal* for figures published July 27, 1957.

The *British Weekly*, the Church of Scotland, and the authors for quotations from James Reid and a prayer by William Barclay.

Miss Adela M. Curtis for quotation from *The Way of Silence*.

The Dohnavur Fellowship, Dohnavur, South India, for quotation From "Have We Not Seen Thy Shining Garment's Hem?" by Amy Wilson Carmichael.

Doubleday and Company, Inc., for "Barter" from *The Dark Cavalier* by Margaret Widdemer. © 1958 by Margaret Widdemer.

Miss M. V. Dunlop for quotations from *Communal Silence* and *Stillness and Strength*.

E. P. Dutton & Co., Inc., for quotation from *The Temple* by W. E. Orchard. Copyright 1918 by E. P. Dutton; renewal © 1946 by W. E. Orchard. Reprinted by permission of the publishers, E. P. Dutton.

Mr. Arthur Guiterman for quotation from "In the Hospital."

W. Heffer and Sons Ltd. for quotation from "Well know I that, given one trusting heart" by J. S. Hoyland.

Hodder and Stoughton Ltd. for quotation from *Personal Faith Through Personal Freedom* by W. Fearon Halliday.

The Rev. Francis B. James and the *Methodist Recorder* for quotation from the issue of November 15, 1956.

The Rev. James Mackay for "Enter This Door."

Macmillan and Co. Ltd. for quotation from the translation of *Amiel's Journal* by Mrs. Humphry Ward.

Macmillan and Co. Ltd. and Miss Anna Bunston de Bary for "Under a Wiltshire Apple Tree."

Macmillan and Co. Ltd. and Ralph Hodgson for "The Mystery" from *Poems*.

Macmillan and Co. Ltd. and Dr. Edward MacLysaght for quotations from "Test of Faith," "Beyond the Farthest Horizon," and "The Penalty of Love" by S. R. Lysaght.

Macmillan and Co. Ltd. and the trustees of Rabindranath Tagore for quotation from *Gitanjali*.

Miss Helen Macnicol for quotation from Nicol Macnicol's translation "One Who Is All Unfit to Count."

The *Methodist Recorder* for quotation from the issue of July 11, 1957.

The Methodist Youth Department for "For the Strength of His Body" from *Youth at Worship* by Godfrey Pain.

Methuen and Co. Ltd. and the author's executors for quotation from "Christopher Robin Is Saying His Prayers," from *When We Were Very Young* by A. A. Milne.

Methuen and Co. Ltd. for quotation from *The House of the Soul* by Evelyn Underhill.

Bishop Moule's trustees for "Come in, O Come! The Door Stands Open Now" by Handley C. G. Moule.

The Rev. Dr. W. E. Stangster for "Lord Jesus, I Am Longing."

Charles Scribner's Sons for "As the Marsh-Hen Secretly Builds on the Watery Sod," from *The Marshes of Glynn* by Sidney Lanier.

Charles Scribner's Sons for "These Are the Gifts I Ask" by Henry van Dyke. Reprinted from *The Poems of Henry van Dyke* by permission of Charles Scribner's Sons. Copyright 1911 Charles Scribner's Sons.

Sidgwick & Jackson Ltd. and the author's representative for the poem "The Prayer" from *The Collected Poems of John Drinkwater.*

Mr. Siegfried Sassoon for "When I'm Alone," published by Faber and Faber Ltd.

The Society of Authors for quotation from *St. Joan* by Bernard Shaw.

The S.C.M. Press Ltd. for quotations from *A Book of Prayers for Students;* from *The Notebooks of Florence Allshorn,* by J. H. Oldham; from prayers by Dr. A. Herbert Gray and from a prayer by Malcolm Spencer.

The Syndics of the University Press, Cambridge, for quotation from the poem "Expectans Expectavi" from *Marlborough and Other Poems* by C. H. Sorley.

Toc H for "Here Is a Quiet Room" by Donald Cox, from *Witness of a Wayfarer to Talbot House.*

The executors of H. G. Wells's estate for quotation from *The Soul of a Bishop,* published by Cassell and Co. Ltd.

DEDICATED

to

MIG and TONY

PREFACE

I MUST, however briefly, express my gratitude to those who have helped me to produce, from the basis of my own private Prayer Book, a book which, I hope, others may find of help. I fear that the book is still over-personal and that there is too much about it of what I happen to like. For instance, those users who do not like poetry should certainly not use this book. I have printed very many of my favourite passages, but they may not appeal to others. Some parts of the book were written during fairly long spells in hospital following two surgical operations. I hope that this fact has not influenced the book too much. Perhaps a compensation may be that users who are passing through times of illness, depression, weakness or loneliness may be helped rather than hindered.

The prayers are sometimes in the first person singular and sometimes in the first person plural, but users can easily substitute "I" for "we," or vice versa. The Lord's Prayer is in the first person plural, but the individual uses it without hindrance. I rather hope that here and there a husband and wife, or two close friends, may use the book together, but much of it is too private for use at public gatherings.

I think I could convey the message of this *Private House of Prayer* in the form of a sincere petition: "O God, use my joy in Thee, my need of Thee, my quest of Thee, my failures, my sorrows and my sins to help others to find their way to Thee, the Creator, the King, the Father of us all. Use, I pray Thee, this private house of prayer which I have made for Thee, and make the place of Thy feet glorious. Amen."

LESLIE D. WEATHERHEAD

The City Temple,
London

CONTENTS

A
PRIVATE
HOUSE
OF
PRAYER

PART ONE

VESTIBULE

An Explanation

VESTIBULE

An Explanation

As an appendix to my little book, *A Prescription for Anxiety*, I sketched out a form of praying for busy people and called it, "Everyman's House of Prayer." In the present book this scheme is amplified and the "rooms" furnished for a month. At the beginning are some words which have helped me when prayer seemed futile and barren. At the end is a collection of prayers which I wrote in my preparation for the services at the City Temple, London. I have not wittingly taken material from any unacknowledged source.

Every serious Christian recognises that prayer is essential. We are compelled to admit that it comes easier to some than to others. Perhaps reluctantly we are compelled to admit that to *pray* well demands as much practice and self-discipline as to *play* well on an instrument, and that we have not done much about it. Probably all Christian people pray a little and have some kind of traffic with heaven, even if it is only a faint kind of thanksgiving for, and rejoicing in, the beauties of Nature or the love of a friend. Surely if *all* commerce with heaven ended, the soul would die. Science, at any rate, knows nothing of an organism permanently cut off from its environment and remaining alive. Jesus Himself felt the need of prayer, taught prayer and practised prayer. We cannot leave praying to the experts and say, "Well, prayer isn't much in my line." Jesus lived the kind of life which we, in our best moments, desire. Yet He

5

could not live without communion with God. How, then, can we hope to do without prayer?

Yet many of us have not had much specific instruction. We "say our prayers," but for some it is a matter of the Lord's Prayer and a few petitions, taken perhaps unchanged from childhood's days. Let us honestly ask ourselves what we should do with half an hour if we decided to spend it in prayer. If we can satisfyingly answer the question, nothing more needs to be said. But many have no method. They would like to pray, but they do not know how to go about it. The Roman Catholic has his daily Prime and Compline. The Anglican has his Prayer Book. The Quaker is trained to use a silence, and we can gather help from them all, and yet perhaps not feel at home in any of these disciplines.

I myself felt in great need of a method, the more so as much of my life for some years included a lot of travelling, and I have devised a method of praying which has been of use to me, and I would like to pass it on in case others may find it useful.

Let us think for a moment of our Lord's advice to the men and women of His day: "When thou prayest, enter into thine inner chamber, and having shut thy door, pray to thy Father which is in secret."[1] "Enter into your inner room." I had often pondered over that word, because very few, if any, of His hearers would have an inner room. There is evidence that Jesus Himself lived in a one-roomed house. Did He not speak, for example, of putting the lamp on the lampstand that it might give light to "all that are in the house"?[2] That surely implied a one-roomed house. I am sure Jesus would never use language which only applied to rich folk. Then it dawned on my literal, Western mind, that He meant *an imaginative room.*

6

I want to suggest that, since there is no limit to our imagination, no limited quota of building material, we can have, not just one room but a whole house. I will tell you about my house of prayer and offer you a month in it, and then you can build your own and furnish it with some of the glorious truths and promises of our faith. And you can use this house of prayer whenever you have a mind to do so. It is easy to memorise the names of the rooms, and you can enter any or all of them as you sit in the corner of a railway carriage, or in the bus or Underground on the way to work, or between your home and the station, or even without getting out of bed. This, so far from being lazy, can be a useful place to pray because relaxation is of value and it is easier to relax there. By this method you can give as long or as short a time as you wish to devote to prayer, but, of course, a "room" suggests a place in which you tarry. Do not rush through all the rooms looking for God. He can be found in every one. Some may desire to use some rooms in the morning and leave others—particularly the sixth and seventh—for the evening. Some may have so little time that they can only use one room per day. For myself, I find half an hour before, or just after, breakfast the best time. There are seven rooms in the house and they are all prayer rooms. Here they are, then:

ROOM 1. This is the room in which we *Affirm the Presence of God*. A common objection to prayer is that it "feels like talking to nothing," or that "there is no one there." We cannot engineer feeling, but in the first room let us assert the fact that God is present. This we can do by repeating some of the great texts of the Bible.

All through the Bible God asserts His Presence with His people, and it is real prayer to remember the sentences which recall this to our mind. "Enoch walked with God." "Abraham was the friend of God." To Moses God promised His presence and to Joshua He said, "As I was with Moses, so I will be with thee." David feels he can face the dark valley "for Thou art with me," and our Lord not only promised, "Lo I am with you every day until the end of the world," but promised the Holy Spirit "that He may be with you for ever." In this first room I repeat those great words, "with you." By printing them in italics I have drawn attention to them throughout Part III.

With such passages we "furnish" this room and, of course, we can add to them from the hymn book and the poets.

ROOM 2. When we have asserted the fact of the Presence of God, we can pass into the next room in which we *Praise, Thank and Adore God*. It is a good thing to imagine this room full of morning sunshine, for this is the room of thanksgiving. Each of us has something for which to praise and thank God. Indeed it is a revealing thing to write down a list of those things for which we should thank God. We should adore Him for all He is in Himself—and, as we do so, we should call to mind His attributes and remember His love, His splendour, His power, His beauty, His wisdom, His holiness. Then we can thank Him for the way He has led us and for all He has done for us. We are to keep our mind—in this room, at least—away from our worries and fears and weakness and sins. We will look at them later, but, first of all, let us resolutely turn our minds away from preoccupation with them. First we will look at *God* in this mental room dedicated to Praise, Gratitude and Adoration.

We can furnish this room with hymns like the Te

Deum and other great hymns of praise from the hymn book and the poets.

ROOM 3. Now we are ready for a room, rather dim and shadowy as we enter, but brighter as we move across it to the window. It is the room of *Confession, Forgiveness and Unloading.*

Here we confess our sin, not just in a general way but really being honest. Most of us are sometimes jealous, malicious, unkind, irritable, proud, intolerant, impure. We pull off the slick business deal and feel a little bit ashamed. We disparage another's good name. In a hundred ways we do what we know to be wrong and fail to do what the inner spirit prompts us as right. Terribly often we are indifferent to another's need. Here we recognise and put away from us our secret resentments, our arrogant self-importance, our refusals to forgive, our jealousy and envy, our hate and malice and that terrible desire to hit back, which, if retained, block the entry of God's peace into our hearts. Here we part with the secret fear that our self-esteem is being undermined, or that we shall be found inadequate. If we really are inadequate, we must accept the fact. God understands and accepts us as we are. But, of course, we must not pretend to Him or to ourselves. Nor must we try to make the world think us wiser, or cleverer, or better, or younger (or whatever it is) than we are. All deception blocks the path to God's peace.

But God is always ready and willing to forgive us. We can move towards the window, pull up the blind and let the streaming light of loving forgiveness and acceptance flood the room. We are loved, understood, forgiven and accepted.

In this room part of Psalm 51 would be a suitable

9

piece of furniture; the Psalm in which David pours out his soul to God and finds pardon. Before we leave this room, too, we must make sure that we are ready to forgive others who may have sinned against us. Nothing is clearer in the New Testament than the fact that God asks, as a condition of His forgiveness, not so much a penitence that is complete, as a spirit that will forgive another. "Forgive us our sins, *as we forgive them that trespass against us.*" "If ye forgive not men their trespasses, neither will your Father forgive your trespasses."[1]

Here also we confess our fears and put down our worries and our dark anxieties. They are not necessarily sins. Some of them we cannot help. But here we tell God about them and let the sunshine of His love and purpose shine upon them. Our confusion we put down here, too; our bewilderment as to what we ought to do and which way we ought to go. In this room we tell God everything that troubles us.

ROOM 4 is set aside for *Affirmation and Reception.* Cleansed by forgiveness we are ready now to receive. This prayer of positive affirmation is important. We are no longer to dwell on the depths to which we have fallen, but on the heights to which God will lead us. God is waiting to give. Jesus put the matter in an unforgettable sentence: "All things whatsoever ye pray and ask for, believe that ye have received them and ye shall have them."[2]

So, quietly, with body and mind relaxed, I may say to myself in this room: "The Peace of God is mine. God is giving me His power now. In God I am one with the Spirit of Love. I am caught up into His mighty purposes now. I am safe within His care. The Everlasting Arms

[1] *St. Matthew* 6 15.
[2] *St. Mark* 11 24.

10

are round about me and will not let me fall." Each sentence to be murmured aloud slowly again and again.

The twenty-third Psalm is suitable furniture for this room. It does not ask, "O Lord, be my Shepherd." It affirms that He is. It does not ask for guidance. It rests in the affirmation that the soul is being guided. "He is leading me in a true path for His name's sake and He is restoring my soul." One should say the words quietly and confidently, repeating each sentence over and over again. Some may wish to visit this room just before sleeping at night. I can think of no more valuable way of falling asleep than to do so repeating some great affirmation about God, such as, "I will be quiet, resting in Thee, Thou Spirit of Peace within me." This thought will sink deep into the unconscious mind, creating and storing an inward peace on which to draw on difficult days when the temptation is to take our reaction from the storm around us, to react in bad temper or ruffled feelings, in worry and anxiety, instead of taking our reaction from the stores of peace laid by through prayer for just such occasions.

It might help us to remember that if God were not willing to give, then we could wrest nothing out of His hands. But if He is willing to give, then we have only to take. The Bible says He is more willing to give than we are to ask. How *can* I take? I take by affirming that His love and peace and power are at my disposal, and that His peace is flooding my heart, even while I bow in this inner room.

It is important to remember that the act of Affirmation must not be made merely by the intellect and carried out by the will. One of the causes of spiritual inefficiency is that while mind and will concur—the mind accepting

truth and the will trying to carry out its implications—
yet the deep emotional levels are unreached.

For instance, I may *know* intellectually that resentment is wrong and may even make me ill. I may do my
best by means of my *will* not to be resentful. Yet the
emotion remains. I *feel* resentful.

To alter that condition I must get the opposite,
positive emotion into my deep mind, and to do *that* I
must repeat, a score of times or more, some positive
statement such as, "God is love and His love fills my
heart and overflows to all men, forgiving and loving all
for His sake."

Someone has said that "the subconscious is an ass"
and I think I know what he means. Ideas presented to
it by repetition during relaxation are accepted by it
almost without the intellect being consulted, and the
emotional colour of the deep mind is altered. Coué knew
this and his system rested on its truth. His pupils were
to say the famous words over and over again: "Every
day in every way I am getting better and better." "Say
it parrot fashion," said Coué, and added, with unconscious humour, "Don't think about it. Say it as you say
the Litany."

I myself found immense help from repeating as I
sought to sleep, "Through the inpouring of Thy love,
Thou art healing me of all that is contrary to Thy
Spirit." I believe that the healing process goes on
during sleep for "He giveth unto His beloved in sleep."[1]
Did not Brother Lawrence say, "The barque of the soul
goeth forward even in sleep"?

ROOM 5 is the place for *Purified Desire and Sincere Petition*.
We all know what our dominant desires are. In this

[1] *Psalm* 127 [2] (R.V. margin).

room we purify them by looking at them again in the light of God. Maybe we shall see that in that light our prayer to become manager of the bank, or headmistress of the school, to make money, achieve fame or be a social success is not so important as to be used by God in some way that helps others.

It is found that some of our thoughtless and selfish prayers that begin, "I want," die on our lips by the time we get to this room in the house of prayer. Probably by this time we want to love more deeply both God and our fellows and promote God's interests even more than our own. We stop saying, "Give me," and start saying, "Make me" and "Show me" and "Use me." This is the place where we ask for renewed trust and stronger faith and more tolerant love for those who differ from us.

In a university common room a number of lecturers were chatting together. Someone asked the question, "What do you want to be?" The others replied in turn and the answers were not unworthy. One wanted an academic distinction, another an athletic prize, another a professor's chair. One man, shy and sensitive, said quietly, "You fellows will laugh at me, but I want to be a saint." They did not laugh at him. I know this man and can sincerely add that he *is* a saint and one of the most healthy influences at a large university. When we can sincerely say, "I want to be a saint," we are purifying our petitions.

ROOM 6 is that of *Intercession for Others*. It has never seemed practicable to me to spend a lot of time on each person for whom I wish to pray, and if the other rooms in the house of prayer have been conscientiously visited, it seems enough to me to say the name of the person slowly, calling him to mind in as vivid a picture as possible, and then imaginatively *watching him emerging from his difficulties*; being made well—if we are praying about his health, being made confident, courageous, serene, joyous, or whatever it may be.

The words italicised are very important. Our minds at the moment of intercession can be so filled with pity, or negative sympathy, or fear, or even horror, that we cannot help and may hinder another. Miss M. V. Dunlop writes[1]: "It is the power of our thought for ill that is so overwhelming, the knowledge that by our states of worry, despondency, fear and other forms of faithlessness we are not only laying up a more or less miserable future for ourselves, but—far worse—are making life harder for those we love and want to help; harder because our mental state is actually intensifying their belief in the power of illness or some misery, and so giving their condition a stronger hold over them. We do not always remember that, far from bearing another's burden, we are binding it on more firmly by much of our sympathy. If we did, we should make far more effort to conquer our own 'natural' grief for someone else's affliction than is at all common. The conquest of grief lies not in suppressing it but in holding our minds still before the Lord (to use an old Quaker phrase) till we are filled with the realisation of His Life and Power. Then, and only then, is our longing to help the other and lighten the burden made possible of fulfilment."

I remember a friend of mine asking me *not* to pray for him in church. When I asked why, he said that the feelings of horror which would be called forth when I told the congregation what had happened to him would hurt him more than the prayers would help him. His words pulled me up and made me take greater care

[1] *Stillness and Strength*, p. 29.

about the way in which I described the person for whom public prayers are offered.

My own plan in praying privately for friends is to have four lists numbered one to thirty-one and against each numeral to pencil four names. (See pages 33–4.) Then, on the day of the month I am praying, I think of the four people whose names are opposite the number which represents the date. In this book a space is left at the end of each day's "Room 6" also, so that names can be pencilled in. Of course, some must be mentioned daily and urgent situations will arise. But I have never felt that "God bless all my friends" is a sufficiently focused prayer, nor can I feel much reality in praying for causes. "God bless the Missionary Society," let alone "God bless India," would seem to me less valuable than to think of someone—if possible personally known and whose difficulties are real to one—who is working in that field. By some such plan as this one can really pray for one's friends, if it be only once a month, with some sense of sincerity and reality. Paul said he would "mention" his friends in his prayers.[1] George Macdonald says, "I will not say that I will pray for you, but I shall think of God and you together."

ROOM 7 is a big room at the top of the house set aside for *Meditation*. Here we sometimes take an incident in the Gospels and try to do what Ruskin said he did, "to be present as if in the body at each recorded act in the life of the Redeemer." We might indeed work steadily through the Gospels in this way, imaginatively watching the incidents happen and especially "looking at Jesus." Some examples are given in the following pages and our meditation should end in dedication. The will

---

[1] *Romans* 1 9; *Ephesians* 1 16.

should be strengthened by all that the imagination has contemplated. Some of the Meditations which follow are poems which are worth reading repeatedly and brooding upon.

A suite of rooms for use on a Sunday can be found on pages 272–8.

This sevenfold way may not prove attractive. All that matters is that we should find *some* way of praying that is *real*, and neither dull or burdensome, nor so unarranged and desultory as to waste time and be unrewarding.

We are all troubled by "wandering thoughts." Sometimes it is a good thing to note just where they do wander; to ask why they wander there and to pray about the situation to which they drift.

Sometimes we are like A. A. Milne's Christopher Robin:

God bless Mummy—I know that's right.
Wasn't it fun in the bath tonight?
The cold's so cold and the hot's so hot;
Oh, "God bless Daddy"—I quite forgot.

If I open my fingers a little bit more,
I can see Nanny's dressing-gown up on the door,
It's a beautiful blue, but it hasn't a hood,
Oh, "God bless Nanny and make her good."

It isn't only the child Christopher Robin who experiences this difficulty. Listen to Benjamin Jowett, a famous Master of Balliol College, Oxford: "Nothing makes one more conscious of poverty and shallowness of character than difficulty in praying or attending to prayer. Any thoughts about self, thoughts of evil, day dreams, love fancies, easily find an abode in the mind. But the thought of God and of right and truth will not stay there, except with a very few persons. I fail to understand my own nature in this particular. There is nothing which at a distance I seem to desire more than the knowledge of God, the ideal, the universal; and yet for two minutes I cannot keep my mind upon them. But I read a great work of fiction, and can hardly take my mind from it. If I had any real love of God, would not my mind dwell upon Him?"

The scheme I have devised offers help to wandering minds like my own.

One could, of course, fill the scheme out to last an hour or more, or shorten it to a few minutes. It is really rather fun to gather passages from the Bible, the hymn book, the poets and the essayists and biographers to make more pictures and furniture for each room. One could in time change the pictures and the furniture in every room.

At any rate, I pass on the scheme for what it is worth. We need God. The masters of prayer teach us that all the factors I have mentioned, like adoration, thanksgiving, confession, petition, intercession and meditation, have their place, and yet some of their books are so advanced that they frighten beginners like me.

The order seems important to me. I want to assert first the Divine Presence and realise the fact, if not the feeling, that there is "Someone there." Then I can adore, worship, praise and thank Him. To do that makes me terribly conscious of my own unworthiness, so I turn then to forgiveness and the unburdening of my heart. Having, as it were, emptied my heart, I want to fill it with what God will give me if I *take* it by the method of repeated affirmation. By this time I have passed what I want through the sieve of His will, "through Jesus Christ our Lord," if I may so put it. I ask in a different way and for different things than would have filled my lips if I had burst into His presence with my petitions at the beginning. Some may think it odd to put intercessions for others so late, but it is when I have myself got nearest to God and asked Him in petition to do things for *me* and in *me* that I can be of maximum help to others. Then, last of all, I want to meditate by "looking at Jesus" or contemplating some great truth which has come to me from Him. In this way imaginative communion with Him can have—as nearly as possible—the result of being with Him in Galilee. That communion is surely the strongest transforming power in the world. What it did for Peter and John, it can do for me.

We must each find the way. "God," said Emerson, "enters by a private door into every individual." "Come down Thine own secret stair," cries George Macdonald. But we can help by making an imaginative house with many doors and stairways, and open them all to Him. He will come in His own way and by His own route. As long as God comes it does not matter how, but we must give Him a chance. "Behold," He says, "I stand at the door and knock: if any man hear My voice and open the door, I will come in to him *and will sup with him*, and he with Me"[1]—in the East an unmistakable offer of friendship from which there will never be any turning back.

I have always found prayer difficult. So often it seems like a fruitless game of hide-and-seek where we seek and God hides. I know God is very patient with me. Without that patience I should be lost. But frankly, I have to be

[1] *Revelation* 3 20.

18

patient with Him. With no other friend would I go on seeking with such scant, conscious response. Yet I cannot leave prayer alone for long. My need drives me to Him. And I have a feeling that He has His own reasons for hiding Himself, and that finally all my seeking will prove infinitely worth while. And I am not sure what I mean by "finding." Some days my very seeking seems a kind of "finding." And, of course, if "finding" meant the *end* of "seeking," it were better to go on seeking. I suppose no one ever finds all there is to find or can rest satisfied as if he had arrived at a journey's end. I long for more satisfaction, but I cannot cease from questing. Jesus sometimes found prayer difficult. Some of His most agonised prayers were not answered. But He did not give up His praying. I frankly have little to show for all my prayers, but I cannot give up, for "my soul longeth for God," and I know that outside God there is nothing at all but death.

Let us, then, make a house of prayer and, if possible, open the door every morning, for to commune with Him may well be the cause for which we were created. It is a very private house. We will not open the rooms to another unless he or she is closely allied in desire. There is One Who "seeth in secret."

"When thou prayest," said Jesus, "enter into thine inner room, and when thou hast shut thy door, pray to thy Father Who is in secret. And thy Father Who seeth in secret, shall reward thee openly." A reward, surely, which shall be a new quality of life, full of serenity and joy and love, a worthy reaction to all life's demands, and, in the end, a communion with God worth all our present disappointments; a communion which shall be a tiny part of His own glory and the whole of our bliss.

PART TWO

WHEN THE DOORS
WILL NOT OPEN TO US

What to do when Prayer seems vain

WHEN THE DOORS
WILL NOT OPEN TO US

What to do when Prayer seems vain

NOTE 1
Times of Dryness

THE STRESS of dryness and darkness and what to do then? . . . There is each time, one crucial point—to form no conclusions, to take no decisions, to change nothing during such crises, and especially at such times not to force any particularly religious mood or idea in oneself. To turn gently to other things. . . . What is a religion worth which costs you nothing? What is a sense of God worth which would be at your disposal, capable of being comfortably elicited when and where you please? It is far, far more God Who must hold us, than we who must hold Him. And we get trained in those darknesses into that sense of our impotence without which the very presence of God becomes a snare.

FREDERICH VON HUGEL

NOTE 2
Emotional Reactions

EVEN WHEN we cannot detach ourselves sufficiently from our surroundings to meditate properly, we can drop (positive affirmations) into our minds at frequent intervals. Whenever we are tempted to "go out" emotionally to some occurrence that would seem to have the power to make us afraid, or dejected, or impatient, or faithless in some way, we can meet the temptation by exercising the power of choice. "No, I will not accept my feeling from this event. I will draw it from Thee, Spirit of Holiness within me; and in the Joy and Peace of knowing Thy power of Holiness is with me, I will deal with this situation."

M. V. DUNLOP
Communal Silence

NOTE 3
Dismal Moods

IF YOU have a negative feeling (worry, fear, anxiety, depression, hate, resentment, etc.) and it does not go away when you meditate, you must take immediate action. . . . Instead of sitting down in front of that mood to wrestle with it by denials, *do* an heroic thing, a thing quite against your natural instincts; *make yourself act quickly upon the opposite of that state.* . . . It is easy enough to act kindly if you feel kindly, the thing is to act by what you know to be right, no matter what you feel. . . . The moment you feel any hate or fear or pride, think of the opposite state and act upon it quickly. If you do this, you will find that you overcome the feeling in a wonderful way and you will have more power over the next mood. If you will make one single action you will find the whole thing has begun to change. . . . You can make yourself happy. . . . Practise on anyone. You have no idea of the virtue of acting on what you know is right if you want to overcome your feelings or nerves. There is some fun in it too. It ought to appeal to your sporting instincts.

ADELA M. CURTIS
The Way of Silence

Persistent Anxiety

MOST PEOPLE over fifty, having lived through two world wars and known fear and worry in other ways, will find periods when anxiety holds them in thrall. They expect prayer to help them and positive affirmation sometimes does, but the anxiety may not pass and they may be disappointed in the "failure" of prayer.

Frequently the anxiety—or fear-feeling—will persist without our realising its cause. The cause may be the war, or some long-past incident or series of incidents, which do not rise into consciousness. Some psychologists think that incidents which terrified our ancestors can affect us. This "floating anxiety," as some call it, can attach itself to some comparatively trivial thing, such as a minor phase of ill-health, or having to take a journey, answer a difficult letter, entertain friends, or visit the dentist. At three in the morning, the very worst horrors loom up. We cannot sleep and we become certain we have got cancer, or that husband or wife is unfaithful, or that the dinner-party will be a flop, or that our business will fail. We cannot put out of our minds the thing Mr. or Mrs. So-and-So said or did, nor can we banish our angry resentment about it. It is a help to remember that thousands feel as we do. Hence the immense vogue of tranquillisers.[1]

[1] At the British Medical Association Annual Meeting at Newcastle in 1957, the delegates were told that in 1956 American chemists filled in thirty million prescriptions for tranquillisers compared with ten million the year before. Fifty thousand million tablets of one popular tranquilliser were sold in 1956. Figures in this country were not published, but barbiturate consumption in Britain in 1955 amounted to forty-eight tons at a cost of £2,000,000; a consumption of twenty doses per head of the entire population.

They have their place, but most of us desire to outgrow the need of them. A correspondent wrote to a religious weekly as follows[1]: "I was on the verge of a nervous breakdown, and was walking down Princes Street in Edinburgh after visiting a specialist, when I met my own doctor, in town for a meeting, who asked me why I was there. I told him. 'A sheer waste of your time and money,' he said. 'Let me talk to you frankly. There is no doctor and no medicine on earth that can do you any good, but you will cure yourself if you take the advice you have often heard from another source, and get into the habit of living a day at a time, and not trying to carry today the burdens of your tomorrows. Besides that, smile at yourself every morning in your mirror when you have finished shaving, and keep smiling the rest of the day. You can't be miserable inside when you keep a smile on your face; it sinks in and down. Do this, and you'll be a different man in a year.' I was in a month, and have remained so to this day."

Alas! some of our troubles are too deep to be remedied so easily, and I believe intensely in the value of the work of the Christian psychiatrist, but the advice above is worth trying.

"A man," says Dr. James Reid, "who had a nervous breakdown, was treated by an expert for two years and then was able to return to work. But he was still liable to periodic attacks of acute anxiety. Prayer did not seem to help. A friend to whom he went in one of his dark moments suggested that he switch his mind from his anxieties and make a complete commitment of himself to God, even though it might mean that he had to *accept his recurrent fear as a wounded soldier accepts his disability.*

[1] *Methodist Recorder*, July 11th, 1957.

26

The result was a gradual, but in the end a total, release."[1]

We must, of course, focus our mind on God's will for that day as far as we can discern it. *We must not substitute for this, setting matters right according to our own idea of what our lives should be like.*

"How can we thank God," asks John Casteel, "for the joys and benefits we receive if basically we are fearful and resentful towards having to live at all, or if we insist on using our capacities, resources and opportunities to inflate and gratify our own self-centred will rather than as means by which we might realise God's will for us? . . . How can we seek the help and mercy of God for ourselves and others if we still harbour hostility to Him for having created us, or towards other people whom we hold accountable for our predicament?"[2]

And let us realise that "accepting the will of God" means contented acceptance, not just resigning ourselves to personal disappointment.

NOTE 5

Faith and Fear

IT IS quite untrue and terribly unkind to suppose that Christians who are sometimes anxious have no faith. Sensitive people of so-called highly-strung natures show fear when the somnolent and phlegmatic see no cause for it and can imagine none. Jesus in Gethsemane showed the extremity of fear and worry, and wanted to find a way of escape. "He was appalled and agitated" (the words bear a load of fear which weighs them down with meaning to the waterline) and He said, "If it be possible let this cup pass." The disciples slumbered on. Were they

---

[1] *British Weekly*, November 29th, 1956 (italics mine).
[2] John Casteel, *Rediscovering Prayer*, p. 57 (Hodder & Stoughton).

braver? Of course not! They were unimaginative and insensitive. We may not have to face a Gethsemane, but we have our own trials, and it is no help to be called coward by implication, or faithless by those whose natures are built on a different plan.

Further, many, like myself, had fears sown in their hearts during childhood, and have never escaped a certain amount of domination by them or found complete release from them. Just as a child, wounded in the body by some accident or ill-treatment, may limp for life, so a child, assaulted by fear in tender childhood and not treated properly, may mentally, or rather, emotionally, limp for life. For myself, if nervously exhausted or even overtired, there sometimes leaps upon the spirit a terrifying fear of something I cannot identify. Many know these nameless terrors and many more know the vague *malaise* of chronic apprehension. They do all they know physically, mentally and spiritually to cope with life, and many act with a bravery as great as that which a battlefield demands. Let no one belittle their faith or doubt their religious sincerity. If some critics had to face what life asks of a neurotic patient, made so, perhaps, by war-wounds in the mind, they would flee the field and escape at least into chronic invalidism.

Those superior people who can always sleep and who say loftily, "I go to bed to sleep," after our confession of a sleepless night, might sometimes ask themselves whether they are paying themselves a compliment. St. Paul, we may comfort ourselves, confessed to "many a sleepless night,"[1] and knew what it was to tremble with fear [2] and to be depressed.[3]

[1] 2 *Corinthians* 11 [27] (Moffatt).
[2] 1 *Corinthians* 2 [3] (Moffatt) and 2 *Corinthians* 7 [5] (Moffatt).
[3] 2 *Corinthians* 1 [8] (Moffatt).

Yet Paul went on praying to be delivered and gave to the world his prescription: "In nothing be anxious; but in everything by prayer and supplication with thanksgiving let your requests be made known unto God. And the peace of God, which passeth all understanding, shall guard your hearts and your thoughts in Christ Jesus."[1]

NOTE 6

When Mystery Blankets Faith

THERE ARE HOURS, and they come to us all at some period of life or other, when the hand of Mystery seems to be heavy on the soul—when some life-shock scatters existence, leaves it a blank and dreary waste henceforth for ever, and there appears nothing of hope in all the expanse which stretches out, except that merciful gate of death which opens at the end—hours when the sense of misplaced or ill-requited affection, the feeling of personal worthlessness, the uncertainty and meanness of all human aims, and a doubt of all human goodness, unfix the soul from all its old moorings—and leave it drifting—drifting over the vast Infinitude, with an awful sense of solitariness. Then the man whose faith rested on outward authority and not on inward life will find it give way: the authority of the priest; the authority of the Church: or merely the authority of a document proved by miracles and backed by prophecy: the soul—conscious life hereafter—God—will be an awful desolate Perhaps. Well! in such moments you doubt all—whether Christianity be true: whether Christ was man or God or a beautiful fable. You ask bitterly, like Pontius Pilate, What is Truth? In such an hour what remains? I reply,

[1] *Philippians* 4 $^{6-7}$.

29

Obedience. Leave those thoughts for the present. Act—be merciful and gentle—honest: force yourself to abound in little services: try to do good to others: be true to the Duty that you know. *That* must be right whatever else is uncertain. And by all the laws of the human heart, by the word of God, you shall not be left in doubt. Do that much of the will of God which is plain to you, and "you shall know of the doctrine, whether it be of God."

F. W. ROBERTSON
Sermons preached at Brighton

George Congreve has a word to add here: "To give way to depression, to face the day's sorrow without hope is to have lost the battle before it begins; it is to betray our cause, to take it out of God's hands and surrender it to the welter of earthly chances. Hope is itself a victory because it is the soul's grasp of God."

We can often hold fast to hope when faith and prayer seem futile and impossible. If this is the best we can do, God will understand, and accept. "Leave it all quietly with God, my soul."

NOTE 7

When Prayer seems a Waste of Time

THE BREAD of prayer is often without taste; the most beautiful thoughts often leave nothing effective in the soul, and sometimes the drynesses pass into powerlessness to meditate. But the soul, in spite of the dryness which has come to it, does not leave its meditation; it goes over and over its material for meditation, and when it can no longer do anything, it resolves to suffer without inquietude, this cross being of greater merit than affections or thoughts. Neither does the contemplative soul abandon its *contemplation* on account of dryness; its nothingness suffices it in the presence of God, and dryness is, after all, in greater conformity with its state of abnegation than consolations and sweetnesses. The faith which upholds it is verily a dry ground, but it is a solid ground on which one can build firmer foundations than on ground wet with rain or dew, in which one's feet sometimes sink down and bring back nothing but mud. Dryness deprives one of thought, but it does not deprive one of the presence of God, even though it can deprive one of the *feeling* of His presence. Faith is never really lost even in the greatest tribulations, and in consequence the presence of God, which nourishes it, endures for ever.

FRANÇOIS MALAVAL
*A Simple Method of Raising the
Soul to Contemplation*[1]

[1] I owe this quotation to Dr. John Baillie's *Diary of Readings* (Nashville: Abingdon Festival Book, 1978).

Daily Intercessions

I pray for:

And I pray for those who await me on the other side.
Especially I think of:

We also bless Thy holy Name for all Thy servants
departed this life in Thy faith and fear; beseeching Thee
to give us grace so to follow their good examples that
with them we may be partakers of Thy heavenly kingdom. Grant this, O Father, for Jesus Christ's sake, our
only Mediator and Advocate. Amen.

The Book of Common Prayer

Intercession List

The names on the lists which follow, together with names on the previous page, could suitably be spaced out and entered in the space devoted daily to Intercession (Room 6)

DAY 1

DAY 2

DAY 3

DAY 4

DAY 5

DAY 6

DAY 7

DAY 8

DAY 9

DAY 10

DAY 11

DAY 12

DAY 13

DAY 14

DAY 15

DAY 16

DAY 17

DAY 18

DAY 19

DAY 20

DAY 21

DAY 22

DAY 23

DAY 24

DAY 25

DAY 26

DAY 27

DAY 28

DAY 29

DAY 30

DAY 31

PART THREE

OPEN HOUSE

A Seven-roomed House of Prayer for a Month

OPEN HOUSE

A Seven-roomed House of Prayer for a Month

The Affirmation of the Divine Presence

WHITHER shall I go from Thy Spirit, or whither shall I flee from Thy presence? If I ascend up into heaven, Thou art there; if I make my bed amongst the dead, behold, Thou art there. If I take the wings of the morning, and dwell in the uttermost parts of the sea; even there shall Thy hand lead me, and Thy right hand shall hold me. If I say, "Surely the darkness shall overwhelm me and the light about me shall be night," even the darkness hideth not from Thee, but the night shineth as the day. The darkness and the light are both alike to Thee.   *Psalm* 139 [7-12]

I here and now affirm the presence of the inescapable God. I here and now rejoice in the presence of the everywhere-available, omnipresent Friend.

Adoration, Praise and Thanksgiving

MY SOUL doth magnify the Lord and my spirit hath rejoiced in God my Saviour. For He hath looked upon the lowliness of His handmaiden. . . . He that is mighty hath done to me great things

AND HOLY IS HIS NAME.

His mercy is unto generations and generations on them that fear Him. . . .

He hath exalted them of low degree. The longing heart (hungry) He hath filled with good things, and the complacent (rich) He hath sent empty away.

St. Luke I 46–53

I adore and praise and give thanks to Thee, O God, because, though I am what I am, Thou art

UTTERLY HOLY.

I adore Thy splendour and I cast myself in lowly worship at Thy feet, awaiting, like Mary, Thy holy will.

This is that blessed Mary, pre-elect
God's virgin. Gone is a great while, and she
Dwelt young in Nazareth of Galilee.
Unto God's will she brought devout respect,
Profound simplicity of intellect
And supreme patience. From her mother's knee
Faithful and hopeful; wise in charity;
Strong in grave peace; in pity circumspect.

So held she through her girlhood; as it were
An angel-watered lily, that near God
Grows and is quiet. Till, one dawn at home
She woke in her white bed, and had no fear
At all,—yet wept till sunshine, and felt awed:
Because the fulness of the time was come.

DANTE GABRIEL ROSSETTI

Confession, Forgiveness and Unloading

HAVE MERCY upon me, O God, according to Thy lovingkindness: according to the multitude of Thy tender mercies blot out my transgressions. Wash me throughly from mine iniquity and cleanse me from my sin. For I acknowledge my transgressions and my sin is ever before me. . . . Purge me with hyssop and I shall be clean; wash me, and I shall be whiter than snow. . . . Hide Thy face from my sins and blot out all mine iniquities. Create in me a clean heart, O God; and renew a right spirit within me. Cast me not away from Thy presence, and take not Thy holy spirit from me. Restore unto me the joy of Thy salvation: and uphold me with a willing spirit. . . . The sacrifices of God are a broken spirit: a broken and a contrite heart, O God, Thou wilt not despise. *Psalm* 51 [1–3, 7, 9–12, 17]

Positive Affirmation and Reception

THE LORD is my Shepherd; I shall not want. He is making me to lie down in green pastures. He is leading me beside the waters of rest. He is restoring my soul. He is guiding me in true paths, for the sake of His name. Yea, though I walk through the valley of the shadow of death I will fear no evil, for Thou *art* with me. Thy rod and Thy staff are giving me comfort. Thou art preparing a table before me in the presence of mine enemies. Thou *hast* anointed my head with oil and my cup *is* running over. Surely goodness and mercy *shall* follow me all the days of my life: and I will dwell in the house of the Lord for ever. *Psalm* 23

I note that the Psalmist says "He" until he speaks about the shadowed valley. Then he says "Thou." He speaks *about* God. Then he turns and speaks *to* God. The Friend has *come* and is *there*.

I note that "hast," that "is" and that "shall." Let me also use the past to fortify the present, and use the past and the present to help me face the future in confidence and in trust. Because of all that God *has* done for me in the past; because He brings me through each day as it becomes the present, let me affirm and receive His power, so that fear for the future may fall away from my heart.

DAY I ROOM 5
Petition

IF INDEED it be necessary, O Lord, to bury the workman that my work may be finished by other hands, help me never to think myself indispensable. May I be content to die with my work undone, knowing that my task is to work AT the fulfilment of Thy purposes, not to work them OUT. s.u.[1]

God buries His workmen, but He carries on His work.
JOHN WESLEY

Let me rest, O God, in the thought that all that matters is that I should rejoice to be Thy child; a child who can never fall out of Thy care, and let me be willing to follow the pathway of Thy will in each circumstance that arises, without chafing to be here or there, or to do this or that.

So, I pray Thee, bring me to the end of this day without dishonour and to my journey's end in peace. Amen.

[1] Source unknown—and so throughout the book.

Intercession

For the Queen, her husband and her family.

For those who are working for the peace of the world.

For all who serve in the Cabinet, in the Lords and Commons.

For all who hold positions of responsibility in universities and colleges.

For all who teach in schools.

For all ministers of the Gospel.

For all fathers and mothers and guardians of children.

For all whose written words in books and newspapers influence the thoughts and actions of others.

All bear responsibility. All contribute either to peace or strife.

Grant, O Lord, that their influence may be used always to bring peace to the world; peace within the Church, peace in the life of the home and peace in the hearts of men.

Thy kingdom come. Thy will be done on earth, as it is in heaven. Amen.

Today I lift up my heart in intercession for:

Meditation

AND HE entered and was passing through Jericho.
And behold, a man called by name Zacchaeus; and
he was a chief publican, and he was rich. And he sought
to see Jesus Who He was; and could not for the crowd,
because he was little of stature. And he ran on before,
and climbed up into a sycomore tree to see Him: for He
was to pass that way. And when Jesus came to the place,
He looked up and said unto him, Zacchaeus, make
haste, and come down; for today I must abide at thy
house. And he made haste, and came down, and
received Him joyfully. And when they saw it, they all
murmured, saying, He is gone in to lodge with a man
that is a sinner. And Zacchaeus stood, and said unto the
Lord, Behold, Lord, the half of my goods I give to the
poor; and if I have wrongfully exacted aught of any
man, I restore fourfold. And Jesus said unto him, Today
is salvation come to this house, forasmuch as he also is
a son of Abraham. For the Son of man came to seek
and to save that which was lost.   *St. Luke* 19 [1–10]

I see this little man who was despised and who despised himself. I watch his undignified ascent of the sycomore tree. I watch and hear Jesus call him. He descends.
Jesus's arm is across his shoulders "brothering" him.
There is no condescension, or heavy attempt to do him
good. Jesus *wants* to be with him: really loves him. All
the Gospel is here. I want Jesus, but, incredibly, *He wants
me*. Jesus utters no word of criticism. Jesus sees the best in
him; a son of Abraham. It is Zacchaeus who judges himself.
So it will ever be. Jesus came not to condemn, but to save,
but in His presence how can I help condemning myself?

Then supper, the unmistakable sign that Jesus wants to be his friend and eat with him. In the east a friendship from which there will be no going back: a friendship which roused holy desire in Zacchaeus and a new determination to lead a different life.

If Jesus did this for Zacchaeus, He will do it for me. He is ever the same. My past life is full of sin, but I do sincerely want Jesus.

I have lost much of my idealism and been content with lower standards. I have lost much of my faith and sometimes I have lost hope. I have lost much of my love for my fellows. I have lost much of my desire to serve them at cost to myself.

Let me meditate upon the wondrous words: "The Son of Man came to seek and to save that which was lost."

Dear Lord, let me have communion with Thee now, and bring the salvation of Thy friendship to my longing heart.

DAY 2 ROOM I   𝔇𝔞𝔶 2

The Affirmation of the Divine Presence

JESUS said, "Lo, I am *with you* every day until the consummation of the age."

St. Matthew 28 20

The promise was *made*, not invented, and it is—as Livingstone said—"the word of a Gentleman of the most sacred and strictest honour." He will keep His word.

It was fulfilled after the Ascension—when "appearances" largely ceased. For us it will not mean vision or voice. It will mean a mind serener because He is standing by;

43

and a mind more tolerant to new ideas. It will mean a heart more loving to others because He loves us; and a heart more sensitive to the love of others through which He touches our lives. It will mean a will dedicated to His service, for He said, "Ye are My friends if ye do whatsoever I have commanded you." He depends on His friends, and the badge of a friend is to do whatsoever needs doing. It will mean a will stronger to accept what has to be accepted and to endure what has to be endured; a will that *comes to terms with*, rather than submits to, the enemies of our inward peace which cannot yet be conquered.

It will mean that every experience of beauty, truth, goodness, love and joy has a new interpretation.

> Whatever stirs my heart and mind
> Thy presence is, my Lord.

I now affirm that presence and claim that promise.

DAY 2 ROOM 2

Adoration, Praise and Thanksgiving

THOU ART the King of Glory, O Christ,
Thou art the Everlasting Son of the Father. . . .
Thou sittest at the right hand of God in the glory of the Father. . . .
Day by day we magnify Thee
And we worship Thy name ever world without end.

Te Deum Laudamus

As I worship I recall that Thy "Name" meant "the expression of Thy nature." To worship is to regard as worthy, of great worth, as worth-while. Help me to "worship Thy name," to keep my sense of values true, to

44

regard as of the highest worth those qualities which express Thy nature.

For those values are established in the Unseen. It is written: "Thou art the King of Glory." Thou art the supreme manifestation of all those qualities which are most worthy and worth-while and which command my praise. "Thou sittest at the right hand of God in the glory of the Father."

Help me, then, day by day to keep these values before my eyes and watch them in Thee. They will be vindicated at last, so day by day may I magnify Thee and worship Thy name both now and evermore in the age that has no end.

Our Father, Who art in heaven, hallowed be Thy name. Amen.

DAY 2 ROOM 3

Confession, Forgiveness and Unloading

SINS unnumbered I confess,
Of exceeding sinfulness;
Sins against Thyself alone,
Only to Omniscience known:

Deafness to Thy whispered calls,
Rashness midst remembered falls,
Transient fears beneath the rod,
Treacherous trifling with my God;

Tasting that the Lord is good,
Pining then for poisoned food;
At the fountains of the skies,
Craving creaturely supplies;

Chilled devotions, changed desires,
Quenched corruption's earlier fires:
Sins like these my heart deceive,
Thee, Who only know'st them, grieve.

O how lightly have I slept
With Thy daily wrongs unwept,
Sought Thy chidings to defer,
Shunned the wounded Comforter;

Woke to holy labours fresh
With the plague-spot in my flesh.
Angel seemed to human sight,
Stood a leper in Thy light.

Still Thy comforts do not fail,
Still Thy healing aids avail;
Patient inmate of my breast,
Thou art grieved, yet I am blest.

O be merciful to me,
Now in bitterness for Thee.
Father, pardon through Thy Son
Sins against Thy Spirit done.

W. M. BUNTING

DAY 2 ROOM 4
Positive Affirmation and Reception

JESUS SAID, "All things whatsoever ye pray and
ask for, believe that ye have received them already
and ye shall have them." *St. Mark* 11 24

I now make a picture in my mind of myself already in possession of what I ask for, for this begins the process by which it becomes mine. Then I thank Him in advance.

Thou canst make me understand,
　　Though I am slow of heart;
Thine in Whom I live and move,
　　Thine the work, the praise is Thine;
Thou art Wisdom, Power and Love,
　　And all Thou art is mine.

CHARLES WESLEY

"Thou art Almighty Goodness within me."

M. V. DUNLOP

DAY 2 ROOM 5
Petition

IF THOU couldst empty all thyself of self,
　Like to a shell dishabited,
Then might He find thee on the ocean shelf
And say, "This is not dead";
And fill thee with Himself instead.

But thou art all replete with very THOU
And hast such shrewd activity
That when He comes, He says, "This is enow
Unto itself—'Twere better let it be,
It is so small and full, there is no room for Me."

T. E. BROWN

Show me, as my soul can bear,
　The depth of inbred sin;
All the unbelief declare,
　The pride that lurks within;

47

Take me, whom Thyself hast bought,
    Bring into captivity
Every high aspiring thought
    That would not stoop to Thee.

CHARLES WESLEY

DAY 2 ROOM 6

Intercession

FOR ALL who seek to heal the sick—doctors, surgeons, dental surgeons, psychiatrists, nurses, osteopaths, physiotherapists, masseurs and other healers.

That they may increasingly realise that by God's own ordinance they are called upon to co-operate with Him. He alone heals. Without His energies in the bodies and minds of men, all their work would be in vain.

That all Christians may recognise that while doctors and others co-operate with God on physical and mental levels, we are all called upon to co-operate on spiritual levels, since God *commands* the obedience of co-operation on all levels, for "without us, God will not, and without God, we cannot."

Let my prayer avail today to let the will of God be done. Thy will be done on earth, as it is in heaven. Amen.

Today I lift up my heart in intercession for:

Meditation

FATHER,
    Well I know that, given one trusting heart,
Silently, unnoticed, far away,
Thy Kingdom comes:

Well I know that men shall never guess
Where was the solitary heart that trusted Thee:

That heart shall dwell unknown,
Remote and quiet and content in Thee:
Yet none the less through *it*,
Through that weak, solitary, foolish heart,
Thy Will of love to save mankind
Shall have been done:

O Father, Father,
Here is all my heart, my mind, my will,
For Thee.

                              J. S. HOYLAND

O teach me, Lord, that I may teach
    The precious things Thou dost impart;
And wing my words, that they may reach
    The hidden depths of many a heart.

O fill me with Thy fullness, Lord,
    Until my very heart o'erflow
In kindling thought and glowing word,
    Thy love to tell, Thy praise to show.

O use me, Lord, use even me.
  Just as Thou wilt, and when, and where,
Until Thy blessed face I see,
  Thy rest, Thy joy, Thy glory share.

FRANCES R. HAVERGAL

Day 3
DAY 3 ROOM I
The Affirmation of the Divine Presence

MOSES SAID, "Who am I . . .?" But God said, "Certainly I will be *with thee*. . . . I am that I am [meaning, 'I will be what I always have been,' or, 'You can depend on Me']. . . . This is My name for ever."

Exodus 3 11, 12, 14, 15

I affirm the presence with me today of the true and faithful and dependable God in Whom men have trusted for thousands of years; in Whom my fathers trusted; in Whom I trust.

He is a path if any be misled;
  He is a robe, if any naked be;
If any chance to hunger, He is bread;
  If any be a bondman, He is free;
  If any be but weak, how strong is He!
To dead men life He is, to sick men health;
To blind men sight, and to the needy wealth;
A pleasure without loss, a treasure without stealth.

GILES FLETCHER
The Excellency of Christ

Adoration, Praise and Thanksgiving

GLORY to our ascended Lord that He is with us
always.

Glory to the Word of God, going forth with His armies
conquering and to conquer.

Glory to Him Who has led captivity captive and given
gifts for the perfecting of His saints.

Glory to Him Who has gone before to prepare a place in
His Father's home for us.

Glory to the Author and Finisher of our Faith; that God
in all things may be glorified through Jesus
Christ,

To Whom be all worship and praise, dominion and
glory; now and for ever and ever. Amen.

Sursum Corda

I kneel not now to pray that Thou
    Make white one single sin,—
I only kneel to thank the Lord
    For what I have not been;

For deeds which sprouted in my heart
    But ne'er to bloom were brought,
For monstrous vices which I slew
    In the shambles of my thought

Dark deeds the world has never guessed
    By hell and passion bred,
Which never grew beyond the bud
    That cankered in my head.

Some said I was a righteous man—
    Poor fools! the gallows tree
(If Thou hadst let one foot to slip)
    Had held a limb for me.

So for the man I might have been
    My heart must cease to mourn,
'Twere best to praise the living God
    For monsters never born:

To bend the spiritual knee
    (Knowing myself within)
And thank the kind, benignant God
    For what I have not been.

HARRY KEMP

So often I have prayed, "Deliver us from evil." Have I ever thanked Thee, O God, for deliverance from all I might have been and done?

DAY 3 ROOM 3
Confession, Forgiveness and Unloading

O LORD JESUS, why can I never come to Thee and look into Thy face without shame? Why do I always know that my feeling of shame in Thy pure presence is the fruit of something done or undone, something thought or said, some lack of love or faith, some failure to be Thy worthy servant? Forgive me. Above all, let not my many failures make me too ashamed to come any more, for that would be final darkness. Lift me up with a love and assurance that make me know that Thou dost still believe in me. Restore the old relationship and let Thy joy and peace flood my heart again. Amen.

Positive Affirmation and Reception

I BELIEVE in Jesus as a perfect revelation of God and the only sure Master for my life.

Because of Jesus, I believe in forgiveness—in the forgiveness of God to man, and from man to man, and from me to anyone who needs my forgiveness.

I believe that love is stronger than all other forces—that to love is better than to be angry, that it is better to give than to receive; better to serve than to be served; better to forget myself than to assert myself.

I believe that God's kingdom *can* come on earth, and that everything that is wrong in the life of the nation, or of the Church, or in my life can be conquered by the power of God.

I believe that nothing that is wrong need be permanent.

A. HERBERT GRAY

I believe in God the Father Almighty, Maker of heaven and earth, and in Jesus Christ, His only Son, our Lord.

The Apostles' Creed

Petition

LORD, I believe in Thee, help Thou mine unbelief. I love Thee, yet not with a perfect heart as I would. I long for Thee, yet not with my full strength. I trust in Thee, yet not with my whole mind. Accept my faith, my love, my longing to know and serve Thee, my trust in Thy power to keep me. I wait Thy blessing. Through Jesus Christ my Lord.

MALCOLM SPENCER

Almighty Father, teach me to do everything with the utmost sincerity. Save me from posing even to myself. Make my life unaffected, simple and sincere. Cleanse me from selfishness; let my gaze be outward rather than inward. Teach me to think more of others than of myself. Forbid that my own interests should be paramount. Pardon, I beseech Thee, all that is and has been wrong in my life and character. . . . Had I always sought Thy will I should now have been strong in the Lord, instead of being the weak, slothful, vacillating creature that I am. But it is never too late. Help me to remedy the evil and henceforth to build with honesty and prayer.

WALTER JAMES

DAY 3 ROOM 6

Intercession

FOR ALL honest seekers after truth, in every denomination, in every religion, and in every phase of human enquiry.

I lift up my heart, O God, for all who earnestly seek for truth and long to find it. As one of them, make me very humble before the majesty of truth and very tolerant of other seekers, even of those who claim to have found it and deny the same claim to others. Grant that I may become more and more sensitive to truth wherever it may be found and through whomsoever it may be offered to me. Especially may I be awake to the danger of rejecting the truth when it comes through people whom I dislike, or whose views on other matters seem to me unsound. Guide me, O Spirit of Truth, to that self-authentication which Thy truth achieves in the heart, and let no fear or dislike deny the authority of that voice of Thine within the soul. Amen.

Today I lift up my heart in intercession for:

DAY 3 ROOM 7
Meditation

AND He must needs pass through Samaria. So He cometh to a city of Samaria, called Sychar, near to the parcel of ground that Jacob gave to his son Joseph: and Jacob's well was there. Jesus therefore, being wearied with His journey, sat thus by the well. It was about the sixth hour. There cometh a woman of Samaria to draw water: Jesus saith unto her, "Give Me to drink." For His disciples were gone away into the city to buy food. The Samaritan woman therefore saith unto Him, "How is it that Thou, being a Jew, askest drink of me, which am a Samaritan woman?" (For Jews have no dealings with Samaritans.) Jesus answered and said unto her, "If thou knewest the gift of God, and Who it is that saith to thee, Give Me to drink; thou wouldest have asked of Him, and He would have given thee living water." The woman saith unto Him, "Sir, Thou hast nothing to draw with, and the well is deep: from whence then hast Thou that living water? Art Thou greater than our father Jacob, which gave us the well, and drank thereof himself, and his sons, and his cattle?" Jesus answered and said unto her, "Everyone that drinketh of this water shall thirst again: but whosoever drinketh of the water that I shall give him shall never thirst; but the water that I shall give him shall become in him a well of water springing up unto eternal life." The woman saith unto Him, "Sir, give me this water, that I thirst not, neither come all the way hither to draw." Jesus saith unto her, "Go, call thy husband, and come hither." The woman answered and said unto Him, "I have no husband." Jesus saith unto her, "Thou saidst well, I have no husband: for thou hast had five husbands; and he whom thou now hast is not thy husband: this hast thou said truly." The woman saith unto Him, "Sir, I perceive that Thou art a prophet. Our fathers worshipped in this mountain; and Ye say, that in Jerusalem is the place where men ought to worship." Jesus saith unto her, "Woman, believe Me, the hour cometh, when neither in this mountain, nor in Jerusalem, shall ye worship the Father. Ye worship that which ye know not: we worship that which we know: for salvation is from the Jews. But the hour cometh, and now is, when the true worshippers shall worship the Father in spirit and truth: for such doth the Father seek to be His worshippers. God is a spirit: and they that worship Him must worship in spirit and truth." The woman saith unto Him, "I know that Messiah cometh [which is called Christ]: when He is come, He will declare unto us all things." Jesus saith unto her, "I that speak unto thee am He."

And upon this came His disciples; and they marvelled that He was speaking with a woman; yet no man said, "What seekest thou?" or, "Why speakest Thou with her?" So the woman left her waterpot, and went away into the city, and saith to the men, "Come, see a Man which told me all things that ever I did: can this be the

Christ?" They went out of the city, and were coming to Him. In the meanwhile the disciples prayed Him saying, "Rabbi, eat." But He said unto them, "I have meat to eat that ye know not." The disciples therefore said one to another, "Hath any man brought Him aught to eat?" Jesus saith unto them, "My meat is to do the will of Him that sent Me, and to accomplish His work. Say not ye, there are yet four months, and then cometh the harvest? Behold, I say unto you, Lift up your eyes, and look on the fields, that they are white already unto harvest. He that reapeth receiveth wages, and gathereth fruit unto life eternal; that he that soweth and he that reapeth may rejoice together. For herein is the saying true, One soweth, and another reapeth. I sent you to reap that whereon ye have not laboured: others have laboured, and ye are entered into their labour."

And from that city many of the Samaritans believed on Him because of the word of the woman, who testified, "He told me all things that ever I did." So when the Samaritans came unto Him, they besought Him to abide with them: and He abode there two days. And many more believed because of His word: and they said to the woman, "Now we believe, not because of thy speaking: for we have heard for ourselves, and know that this is indeed the Saviour of the world."

St. John 4 [4-42]

I can see, in imagination, the sun-drenched scene by Jacob's well. The Master, tired out, has let His men go to the town to buy food while He rests on the edge of the well. Why does the woman come at *noon*? Dawn and dusk are the times to draw water. Is she despised because of her immoral life and therefore finds in the blazing heat more protection than in the cool morning and evening when gossiping women gather and hostile glances hurt? And then she meets Jesus! Jew and Samaritan are supposed to be at daggers drawn, but not this Jew. The courtesies allow Him to ask for *water*, and so the bridge is crossed and the subject of "living water" opened. The woman evades His challenges: "Let's talk about the depth of Jacob's well (11). Let's talk about where men say their prayers (20). Let's talk about the coming Messiah" (25). . . . And then capitulation. Soul to naked soul with no more evasion or beating about the bush. He stayed there two days to see her safely into the kingdom, and "many believed on Him because of the word of the woman" (39) and then found certainty for *themselves*. "We have heard for ourselves and know that this is indeed the Saviour of the world" (42).

Lord Jesus, push past our evasions, and let us sit down quietly face to face with Thee, to acknowledge the hindrances which Thou canst see all the time, pride and self-importance, lust and illicit desire, worry and fear and anxiety about the health of ourselves and our loved ones, about the Church and the future of the world. Lay a forgiving hand upon us now and bring us close to Thee, within Thy kingdom, with all thought of self forgotten—especially self-pity. Oh that we could really *trust* Thee to "bring us conqueror through"! Help us not to run away any longer, but *to relax in entire committal* to Thee, with all doubt banished and all anxiety gone.

Grant that we may know for ourselves, in our own experience, that Thou art indeed the Saviour of the world! Amen.

The Affirmation of the Divine Presence

As I was with Moses, so I will be *with thee*: I will not fail thee, nor forsake thee. Be strong and of a good courage; be not affrighted, neither be thou dismayed, for the Lord thy God is *with thee* whithersoever thou goest . . . only be strong and of a good courage.

Joshua 1 5, 6, 9, 18

DAY 4 ROOM 2

Adoration, Praise and Thanksgiving

My GOD, I thank Thee, who hast made
　　The earth so bright,
So full of splendour and of joy,
　　Beauty and light;
So many glorious things are here,
　　Noble and right.

I thank Thee, too, that Thou hast made
　　Joy to abound,
So many gentle thoughts and deeds
　　Circling us round,
That in the darkest spot of earth
　　Some love is found.

I thank Thee, Lord, that Thou hast kept
　　The best in store;
We have enough, yet not too much
　　To long for more—
A yearning for a deeper peace
　　Not known before.

I thank Thee, Lord, that here our souls,
   Though amply blest,
Can never find, although they seek,
   A perfect rest,
Nor ever shall, until they lean
   On Jesu's breast.

ADELAIDE ANNE PROCTER

Here, in Thy presence, I list those things for which I thank Thee. I thank Thee for:

DAY 4 ROOM 3
Confession, Forgiveness and Unloading

O GOD, Who art seeking ever to weave all my unhappiness into a final pattern of beauty, forgive my rebellion, my resentment, my moods of black despair. I know that I should "accept what cannot be altered," but instead I often chafe and rebel, thinking if only this or that had been, or were to be altered, how happy life could have been, or would still be.

Yet, though I hate the darknesses and fears that oft beset me, and love high spirits, health, success and fun with friends, I have learned more in the darkness than in the light, and I have been pressed nearer to Thy breast by moments of unhappiness and pain than by hours of well-being.

Others suffer, why should not I? . . .

Teach me to accept, to humble myself, to be patient and disciplined, to suffer without self-pity and despair and gloom, remembering that to suffer passes, but what is learned through suffering is treasure for evermore.

O for a closer walk with God,
    A calm and heavenly frame,
A light to shine upon the road
    That leads me to the Lamb. . .

Return, O holy Dove! return,
    Sweet messenger of rest!
I hate the sins that made Thee mourn,
    And drove Thee from my breast.

The dearest idol I have known,
    Whate'er that idol be,
Help me to tear it from Thy throne,
    And worship only Thee.

So shall my walk be close with God,
    Calm and serene my frame;
So purer light shall mark the road
    That leads me to the Lamb.

W. COWPER

DAY 4 ROOM 4
Positive Affirmation and Reception

THOUGH the fig-tree shall not blossom,
Neither shall fruit be in the vines;
The labour of the olive shall fail,
And the fields shall yield no meat;

The flock shall be cut off from the fold,
And there shall be no herd in the stalls:
Yet I will rejoice in the Lord,
I will joy in the God of my salvation.
Jehovah, the Lord, is my Strength.

Habakkuk 3 [17–19]

In other words, though everything goes wrong and I am deprived of all the outward things on which I depend, Thou *art*, and Thou art still Love and Power and Adequacy and Peace.

Though waves and storms go o'er my head,
Though strength, and health, and friends be gone,
Though joys be withered all and dead,
Though every comfort be withdrawn,
On this my steadfast soul relies—
Father, Thy mercy never dies!

J. A. ROTHE
(tr. by John Wesley)

I affirm the reality of that mercy and the adequacy of Thy love and power.

DAY 4 ROOM 5
Petition

TEACH ME, O Lord, to reserve my anger for those things which would anger Thee.

Help me to get my perspective right by my communion with Thee, so that irritating trifles may be seen to be trifling and the irritation allayed; so that injuries done to me may be seen in the perspective of all my injuries to Thee. In the light of Thy patience with, and mercy towards me, help me more readily to forgive others with the genuine restoration of relationship which I claim between myself and Thee.

Lord, let the maintaining of that relationship matter to me more than anything in the world, for in it is my only hope, and in its growing fullness is life both here and hereafter. Amen.

DAY 4 ROOM 6

Intercession

For ALL who are lonely, unhappy or sad. Let the remembrance of all that my friends have meant and mean to me strengthen and make more sincere my intercession for all who are lonely. Let the thought of all the joy I have had in life urge me to pray more earnestly for all who are unhappy or sad today.

For children lonely in boarding schools, frightened amid the crowd of others, terrified of the shadows in the dormitory and the strange noises in the night.

For soldiers, sailors and airmen serving their country far from home and dear ones, looking fondly at photographs of wife and child, or of parents or sweethearts, and longing for the companionship of those dear to them.

For old folk; those who have lost a life-partner, whose children have married and gone far away; and especially elderly women who have never married and for whom uneventful days pass in a grey monotony, and evening hours drag on leaden feet with no cheery word from another and no bright face of a dear one to dispel the darkness of loneliness.

Lord God, I pray for all the lonely and the sad. Brighten their lives. Send them those who can minister

to them. Grant them the direct grace of Thy Holy Spirit.
And help me to answer my own prayers and never to
neglect the lonely ones. For Thy Name's sake. Amen.

Today I lift up my heart in intercession for:

DAY 4 ROOM 7

Meditation

AND WHEN He entered again into Capernaum after
some days, it was noised that He was in the house.
And many were gathered together, so that there was no
longer room for them, no, not even about the door: and
He spake the word unto them. And they come, bringing
unto Him a man sick of the palsy, borne of four. And
when they could not come nigh unto Him for the crowd,
they uncovered the roof where He was: and when they
had broken it up, they let down the bed whereon the sick
of the palsy lay. And Jesus seeing their faith, saith unto
the sick of the palsy, "Son, thy sins are forgiven." But
there were certain of the scribes sitting there, and
reasoning in their hearts, Why doth this Man thus speak?
He blasphemeth: who can forgive sins, but one, even
God? And straightway Jesus, perceiving in His spirit that
they so reasoned within themselves, saith unto them,
"Why reason ye these things in your hearts? Whether is
easier, to say to the sick of the palsy, Thy sins are forgiven; or to say, Arise, and take up thy bed, and walk?
But that ye may know that the Son of man hath power

on earth to forgive sins (He saith to the sick of the palsy), I say unto thee, Arise, take up thy bed, and go unto thy house." And he arose, and straightway took up the bed, and went forth before them all; insomuch that they were all amazed, and glorified God, saying, "We never saw it on this fashion."

St. Mark 2 [1-12]

In imagination I watch these four men, bringing their youthful friend on the stretcher to Jesus. Perhaps the courtyard, with flat-roofed, one-storey buildings on all four sides, was covered over with some temporary roofing to provide shelter from storm and sun for the crowds who always gathered where Jesus was. Unable to get near Jesus in any normal way, they climb the stone stairs which led from the street to the flat rooftops, removed part of the temporary roofing over the courtyard and let the stretcher down. I see the hope in the patient's face. I see the compassion in the eyes of Jesus. I sense the atmosphere of optimism which the four men bring. ("HE seeing THEIR faith. . . .") Christ's word is not of healing, but of forgiveness. How many disabilities of ours would disappear if we could really *feel* completely forgiven, utterly free from guilt? How hard it is thus to feel! How easy, perhaps, if we could look into the loving eyes of Christ!

Lord Jesus, use my faith in Thee to succour and heal those whom I bring to Thee, and if, dear Lord, I myself feel sick at heart and in despair of being whole, then do Thou speak the word of pardon so that I really *receive* it, and so that guilty fear really dies.

My chains fell off, my heart was free,
I rose, went forth and followed Thee.

O that Thou would'st make those words true for me this day. Help me now to see myself not as a poor, whimpering sinner, but as a forgiven son, wearing the robe of sonship and accepted and beloved; a new creature through Thy pardoning grace. So let me hold up my head again, hearing Thee say to me also: "Thy sins are forgiven thee." Amen.

𝕯ay 5   DAY 5 ROOM 1

The Affirmation of the Divine Presence

I HEARD a great voice out of the throne saying, "Behold, the tabernacle of God is with men, and He shall dwell *with them*, and they shall be His peoples, and God Himself shall be *with them* and be their God: And He shall wipe away every tear from their eyes; and death shall be no more; neither shall there be mourning, nor crying, nor pain any more." (The word for "pain" can mean weariness or anxiety.) The first things are passed away. And he that sitteth on the throne said, Behold, I make all things new.   *Revelation* 21 ³⁻⁵

DAY 5 ROOM 2

Adoration, Praise and Thanksgiving

OPEN WIDE the window of our spirits and fill us full of light; open wide the door of our hearts, that we may receive and entertain Thee with all our powers of adoration and love.   CHRISTINA ROSSETTI

We thank Thee, O Lord, for all those good things which are in our world and in our lives through Thy love. Save us from being ungrateful. Save us from magnifying our sorrows and forgetting our blessings. Give strength of spirit to rise into joyfulness of heart. By Thy help may we learn to live as those should who have trusted the promises of good which are incarnate in Jesus, and who know that in the end love must conquer all.

A. HERBERT GRAY

We worship and adore Thee, O God. We praise Thee for being what Thou art. We thank Thee for every glimpse we have of Thy nature and, above all, for the disclosure of Thyself in Jesus Christ our Lord. Amen.

DAY 5 ROOM 3

Confession, Forgiveness and Unloading

ONE THING I of the Lord desire—
    For all my way hath miry been—
Be it by water or by fire,
    O make me clean!

If clearer vision Thou impart,
    Grateful and glad my soul shall be;
But yet to have a purer heart
    Is more to me.

Yea, only as the heart is clean,
    May larger vision yet be mine,
For mirrored in its depths are seen
    The things divine.

I watch to shun the miry way,
    And staunch the spring of guilty thought;
But, watch and wrestle as I may,
    Pure I am not.

67

So wash Thou me without, within;
  Or purge with fire, if that must be—
No matter how, if only sin
  Die out in me.

WALTER CHALMERS SMITH

DAY 5 ROOM 4
Positive Affirmation and Reception

I THANK Thee that, by the inpouring of Thy love, Thou art healing me of all that is contrary to Thy Spirit.

M. V. DUNLOP

Help me now to be quiet, relaxed and receptive, accepting the thought of Thy healing grace at work, deep within my nature.

DAY 5 ROOM 5
Petition

ALMIGHTY God, unto Whom all hearts be open, all desires known, and from Whom no secrets are hid; cleanse the thoughts of our hearts by the inspiration of Thy Holy Spirit, that we may perfectly love Thee and worthily magnify Thy holy name. Through Christ our Lord. Amen.

The Book of Common Prayer

Intercession

FOR ALL who are frightened and unhappy and nervously ill.

I lift up my heart, O God, for all who are the prey of anxious fears, who cannot get their minds off themselves and for whom every demand made on them fills them with foreboding, and with the feeling that they cannot cope with all that is required of them.

Give them the comfort of knowing that this feeling is illness, not cowardice; that millions have felt as they feel, that there is a way through this dark valley, and light at the end of it.

Lead them to those who can help them and understand them and show them the pathway to health and happiness. Comfort and sustain them by the loving presence of the Saviour Who knows and understands all our woe and fear, and give them enough courage to face each day, and rest their minds in the thought that Thou wilt see them through. Amen.

Today I lift up my heart in intercession for:

Meditation

ONE September morning during a stay at "Jordans," the Quaker settlement in Buckinghamshire, I got up at a quarter to seven, walked through the kitchen garden, up through the orchard where the owls were still crying, through a gate and into a meadow. But not only into a meadow, into a great silence. It was in the meadow that I met God. The ground was so drenched with dew that it looked as if it were covered with hoar frost. The sun was peeping over the horizon, throwing long shadows upon the grass. It was an hour of bewitching loveliness. Magic was in the air and awe in my heart. One had that strange impression that one was seeing the world all new and fresh from God's hand. There was a solemn hush which seemed to fall over the whole field and everything in it.

In a way it was a strange experience. One does not *plan* such hours when one goes away for a summer holiday. Yet at the end of that holiday, having done, perhaps, all the things one planned to do, the thing that stands out most is an unplanned hour of silence when the soul was caught up in rapturous worship and allowed to behold part of the beauty of God. One knows that God is near, that He is speaking to one, that He has brought one to that hour and to that place, in order to say things to one in the silence that otherwise one would not stay to hear.

I had a similar experience some years ago after speaking in Lincoln. I did not know who was going to be my host, but after the meeting, which was very hot, very noisy and very uncomfortable, a simple-hearted farmer came up, almost shyly, and said that he was to be my host. He apologised for not having a motor-car. If only he could have known how my heart exulted as we bowled through the narrow lanes in a gig! I felt like a child in fairyland. The gig lamps lit the chestnut haunches of the mare, threw strange, thrilling shadows on the hedgerows and the lower branches of the trees, and frightened here and there a chattering blackbird from its roost. We drew up with a glorious clatter of hoofs on the cobbles of a farmyard. I felt that it had all happened before, perhaps a hundred years ago. One has that feeling sometimes. Men shouted and ran to the unharnessing, and then supper followed in a huge kitchen with a mighty fire. Hams hung from the ceiling. Dogs pushed their noses into one's hand in friendly welcome. The kettle sang on the hearth. A great black and yellow cat sprawled on an oak settee in the chimney corner. We sat down to a white wooden table scrubbed as clean and spotless as linen could be. Then followed cheerful talk, and then the never-to-be-forgotten experience. I was led to a bedroom filled with moonlight and the fragrance of lavender sheets. The bedroom window was thrown up, and when I was alone I knelt at the open window and the sound that thrilled me was the sound of a very distant train being shunted. Chug, chug, chug . . . then a lot of quick "chugs" together. It sounds foolish to say that one was thrilled by the sound of a train, however far off. But the fact is that sounds of that kind *interpret* the silence. They alone make one apprehend how utterly still and quiet is the night. The silent majesty of that moonlight night, lying upon the hushed fields like the supernatural glory of God, needed some gentle sound to interpret and emphasise it. Then the second interpreting sound—also far away— a village clock striking twelve. I shall never forget that night. I felt so wrapped in the presence of God that I did not want to lose it in sleep.

71

I felt that I understood a little better that strange experience of Elijah. After the wind and the earthquake and fire, he heard "a still small voice," or if we interpret more literally, "a sound of gentle stillness."[1] The sound interpreted the silence. How often the hour of the soul's exaltation is an hour of silence!

Some words of Pascal come to the mind in this regard. "All the evils of life," he said, "have fallen upon us because men will not sit alone quietly in a room."

The Significance of Silence

Said James Russell Lowell:

If chosen souls could never be alone,
In deep mid-silence, open-doored to God,
No greatness ever had been dreamed or done.

Make this room of meditation a room of silence, dear Lord, in which I can feel Thy presence and hear Thy voice.

. . . Jesus knelt to share with Thee
The silence of eternity,
    Interpreted by love.

Drop Thy still dews of quietness,
    Till all our strivings cease;
Take from our souls the strain and stress,
And let our ordered lives confess
    The beauty of Thy peace.

[1] *1 Kings* 19[12] (R.V. margin).

Breathe through the heats of our desire
    Thy coolness and Thy balm;
Let sense be dumb, let flesh retire;
Speak through the earthquake, wind, and fire,
    O still small voice of calm!

JOHN GREENLEAF WHITTIER

DAY 6 ROOM 1   𝕯𝖆𝖞 6

The Affirmation of the Divine Presence

THE LORD stood above (Jacob's ladder) and said, "Behold, I am *with thee* and will keep thee whithersoever thou goest. . . . I will not leave thee until I have done that which I have spoken to thee of. . . ." And Jacob said, "Surely the Lord is in this place; and I knew it not. . . . This is none other but the house of God, and this is the gate of heaven."

Genesis 28 13, 15-17

I shall be alone as my Master was. I am hated by some who loved me once, not for what I do, but for what I think. I have long foreseen it. And knowing that my Father is *with me*, I am not afraid to be alone, though, to a man not urgently made, there is some sharpness in the thought. . . . I am alone now and shall be till I die, but I am not afraid to be alone in the majesty of darkness which His Presence peoples with a crowd. . . . A sublime feeling of a Presence comes about me at times which makes inward solitariness a trifle to talk about.

F. W. ROBERTSON
Life and Letters of F. W. Robertson

73

Adoration, Praise and Thanksgiving

JESUS, preaching good tidings to the poor,
    proclaiming release to the captives,
    setting at liberty them that are bound,
            I adore Thee.

Jesus, Friend of the poor,
    Feeder of the hungry,
    Healer of the sick,
            I adore Thee.

Jesus, denouncing the oppressor,
    instructing the simple,
    going about doing good,
            I adore Thee.

Jesus, Teacher of patience,
    Pattern of gentleness,
    Prophet of the kingdom of heaven,
            I adore Thee.

A Book of Prayers for Students

Confession, Forgiveness and Unloading

DEAR MASTER, in whose life I see
All that I would, but fail to be,
Let Thy clear light for ever shine,
To shame and guide this life of mine.

Though what I dream and what I do
In my weak days are always two,
Help me, oppressed by things undone,
O Thou, whose deeds and dreams were one!

JOHN HUNTER

Lord Jesus, Whose loving heart and dedicated mind were focused always on others, give me this day Thy spirit, so that in trying to make others happy and increase their joy, I may be loosed from the burden and load of my own troubles and forget myself. I ask it in Thy name. Amen.

DAY 6 ROOM 4
Positive Affirmation and Reception

THOU ART giving me, here and now, inward peace and complete relaxation and a mind turned towards Thyself.

Jesus said, "Have faith in God." Therefore it must be possible, and is made possible by affirmation, and by acting as though it were possessed already.

Jesus said, "Fear not." Therefore it must be possible, and is made possible by affirmation, by acting as though one were not afraid.

Jesus said, "My joy I give unto you." I accept His gift. I am going to enjoy today and not let it be spoiled by apprehension about an unknowable future, by the demons of fear and worry, by grumbling or self-pity.

Jesus said, "All things whatsoever ye pray and ask for, believe that ye have received them and ye shall have them."

St. Mark 11 24

Petition

GRANT unto us, Almighty God, in all time of sore distress, the comfort of the forgiveness of our sins. In time of darkness give us blessed hope, in time of sickness of body give us quiet courage, and when the heart is bowed down and the soul is heavy and life is a burden and pleasure a weariness . . . then may that Spirit, the Spirit of the Comforter, come upon us, and after our darkness may there be the clear shining of the heavenly Light; that so, being uplifted again by Thy mercy, we may pass on through this our mortal life with patient hope and unshaken trust, certain through Thy loving kindness and tender mercy of being delivered from death into the larger life of the eternal years. Through Jesus Christ our Lord. Amen.

GEORGE DAWSON
(altered)

Intercession

FOR ALL missionaries abroad, remembering their loneliness; the difficulties of language, different customs and strange food; the depression that may sometimes overshadow them and the longing in many of them to have their dear ones near them.

The weary one had rest, the sad had joy that day,
    And wondered how.
A workman whistling at his work, had prayed,
    "Lord, help them now."

Away in foreign lands they wondered how
    Their feeble words had power.
In England, Christians, two and three, had met
    To pray an hour.

Yes, we are always wondering, wondering how,
    Because we do not see
Someone, unknown perhaps, and far away,
    On bended knee.

FRANCES N. NESBITT

Give me faith to believe that my caring can be used by Thee to release into their lives what Thou, the All-Seeing and the All-Loving, knowest they need.

To-day I lift up my heart in intercession for:

DAY 6 ROOM 7

Meditation

WE HAVE dreamed dreams beyond our compre-
    hending,
Visions too beautiful to be untrue;
We have seen mysteries that yield no clue,
And sought our goals on ways that have no ending. . . .
We have seen loveliness that shall not pass
We have beheld immortal destinies; . . .
Ay, we whose flesh shall perish as the grass
Have flung the passion of the heart that dies
Into the hope of everlasting life. . . .
But lo! remains the miracle supreme,—
That we, whom Death and Change have shown our fate,

We, the chance progeny of Earth and Time,
Should ask for more than Earth and Time create,
And, goalless and without the strength to climb,
Should dare to climb where we were born to grope;
That we the lowly could conceive the great,
Dream in our dust of destinies sublime,
And link our moments to immortal hope. . . .
So, let us turn to the unfinished task
That earth demands, strive for one hour to keep
A watch with God, nor watching fall asleep,
Before immortal destinies we ask.
Before we seek to share
A larger purpose, a sublimer care,
Let us o'ercome the bondage of our fears,
And fit ourselves to bear
The burden of our few and sinful years.
Ere we would claim a right to comprehend
The meaning of the life that has no end
Let us be faithful to our passing hours,
And read their beauty, and that light pursue
Which gives the dawn its rose, the noon its blue,
And tells its secret to the wayside flowers.

SIDNEY ROYSE LYSAGHT
Beyond the Farthest Horizon

Day 7

DAY 7 ROOM I
The Affirmation of the Divine Presence

THE ONLY way I can learn it (to practise the Presence of God) is to do it, and one thing I am very sure of for myself is that to sit quietly before God doing nothing, only fixing the will gently on some expressive word like

"O God, I want Thee," or "Father," or "Here am I and here are You," makes a world of difference. Just as lying in the sun doing nothing, surrendering your body to it, with the sun blazing down on you, affects your body and your senses, so this surrendering of the soul to that transforming Power affects the soul, and I believe that as truly as the sun changes the colour of your skin so that Power changes you at the centre.

J. H. OLDHAM
Florence Allshorn

I want to feel gay like Christ felt when people are trying to get one down. He is feeling, "I am with My Father—not with the little devils in your spirit that make you unhappy." *Ibid.*

And the Father's name is Love, Joy, Peace, Serenity, Quietness, Patience, Endurance, Courage, Wisdom, Holiness, Strength, Unselfishness.

This Loving Spirit is with *me*, today.

DAY 7 ROOM 2
Adoration, Praise and Thanksgiving

O GOD, Who art the Truth, O God, Who art Spirit, help me in spirit and in truth to worship Thy great name, not acknowledging Thee in one place or at one time only, but in every place and at every time, in all I do and in all I see, in my work and in my rest, in my laughter and in my tears, in loneliness and in fellowship, in the eye of day and in the shadow of night, beneath the open sky as in the house of prayer, in the heart of the little child, as in the wisdom of the man, in the fulness of health and strength and happiness, as in the valleys of pain and grief and fear, and even in the valley of the shadow of death, through which, O Father Almighty, do Thou in Thy mercy bear me to never-ending life and light and love.

s.u. (altered)

DAY 7 ROOM 3
Confession, Forgiveness and Unloading

IF MY soul has turned perversely to the dark;
If I have left some brother wounded by the way;
If I have preferred my aims to Thine;
If I have been impatient and would not wait;
If I have marred the pattern drawn out for my life;
If I have cost tears to those I loved;
If my heart has murmured against Thy will,
      O Lord, forgive.

F. B. MEYER

If there are tracts of my life into which Christ is not allowed to come; O Lord, forgive, and help me to know more exactly what is Christ's will for me and to yield myself afresh to Him. *A Book of Prayers for Students*

O God, when I think of my sins I know that men have been sent to prison, shamed and ruined, and their families involved in their disgrace, for sins which in Thy sight are no worse than mine. I blush to think of them and wonder at Thy mercy. Forgive me and let me prove my gratitude for Thy forgiveness by sympathy and service for others in humility and love. Amen.

DAY 7 ROOM 4
Positive Affirmation and Reception

I WILL put My Spirit in you and you shall *live*.

M. V. DUNLOP
(based on Ezekiel)

It shall be "put," that is, given. We have not to strive or struggle for it. Our part is to open ourselves to prepare the way of the Lord by our receptiveness, to hold ourselves as channels for the inflowing of Spirit.

His is the Spirit of Holiness—Wholeness or Health of Body, Mind and Spirit. His is the Spirit of Love—and Joy—and Peace—and Humility—and Unselfishness—and Kindness—and Service.

As I repeat these words which are wholly true of Him, I absorb a tiny bit of their essence into my being, and in so doing allow Him more and more dominion in my heart.

DAY 7 ROOM 5
Petition

FILL US, we pray Thee, with Thy light and life, that we may show forth Thy wondrous glory. Grant that Thy love may so fill our lives that we may count nothing too small to do for Thee, nothing too much to give, and nothing too hard to bear. So teach us, Lord, to serve Thee as Thou deservest, to give and not to count the cost, to fight and not to heed the wounds, to toil and not to seek for rest, to labour and not to ask for any reward save that of knowing that we do Thy will. Amen.

IGNATIUS LOYOLA

Intercession

FOR ALL children of every race who suffer from hunger, from physical or mental illness, from cruelty, from lack of love and security.

May my prayer strengthen and assist their angels who always behold the face of the Father.

Lord Jesus, Who didst love little children and Who taught us that of such is the kingdom of heaven, show us new ways of protecting them and a new determination to care for the children of all nations, that, growing up to know and love Thee, they may make the world more like Thy plan for it. So may Thy will be done on earth as it is in heaven. Amen.

Today I lift up my heart in intercession for:

Meditation

THE TRANSFIGURATION

WE IMAGINE Jesus toiling at eventide up the lower slopes of Hermon with the main peak towering beyond Him, lifting its massive head nine thousand feet towards the stars. Having gained the summit of one of its spurs, He stops to pray. Far in the west glows the last gleam of sunset, pale green behind the mountains.

Tremblingly the stars steal into the sky. Silently the darkness surges into valley and glen below them. Like the peace of God on a troubled heart, night descends upon the hills. All through the long day the mountain has sweltered in the burning sun. One imagines that it has longed for the quiet hours of night as wearied eyes watch for the morning. And now, all silently there steals down upon it a long, white, fleecy cloud. Very quietly the cloud, like a white, fleecy blanket put by a tender mother's hand about her fretful, fevered child, gathers around the mountain's form, and it is as though the mountain sighs with some deep inward content and turns to sleep.

And He, its Lord and Lover, kneels upon its warm heather to pray. He is so young to die. His body is strong, not old and weak and ill. His nerves are steel cable, not frayed and shattered with pain or worry or age. His hold on life is strong, so strong! Can it be that the only way He can prove His love is to die? Thoughts of life and love and laughter race through His brain. He can see the village street of Nazareth. He can hear the soft voice of Mary that caressed His babyhood. He can hear the laughing voices of boys at the games they played together. He can see the eyes of John, His close friend, full of worship and wonder. He can hear the ring in Peter's voice: "Thou art the Christ, the Messiah, the One Who should come and deliver our nation." Life is very rich—very sweet. Dear God, how sweet! Blue and gold mornings among the wild anemones on the peaceful hills of Nazareth. Moonlight nights on the lake thinking thoughts of God while His men fished. Bird song and sunshine. Starlight and the hush of night. Health, friendship, the love of little children and the great message yet to be more and more fully declared.

How *can* He leave it all, give Himself to derisive Pharisees, cool, cunning, calculating enemies who will kill Him and say, "There you are, nails will kill Him just like anyone else. It has just been one other in the list of religious and political uprisings and our power has put it down like the rest. It will all be forgotten in six months"?

Jesus's eyes are wet with tears. Great convulsive sobs burst from His breast. He bows Himself lower, till at last Mother Earth, that great Mother of all flesh, takes His prone form and gathers it to her quiet breast, and Night, like some great, pitying Angel, stoops lower and lays her cool hand upon His flushed brow. The great serenity whose name is God possesses Him. He knows that pain and death can be God's angels, and weave all human woe into a divine pattern that will satisfy the soul at last.

Only one thing further He needs. Some comforting assurance that all will be well, some voice of evidence that all that has passed has not been wholly and solely in the world of feeling. He lifts His face. Serenity has become radiance. The glory of the eternal within Him illumines Him with the light that never was on sea or land. It shines in His eyes. His face glows. His very clothes are luminous. And the assurance He needs is at hand. "There appeared unto them Elijah with Moses, and they were talking with Jesus."

The disciples have been asleep. They had walked far and stumbled up a mountain in the dark. The warm heather was too much for them. They wake to see that Transfigured Face. They are at the verge of the universe, which, as yet, man cannot bear. Ghostly presences terrify them. "They fell on their faces and were sore afraid." Practical Peter stammers about three shelters. It is cold on the spurs of Hermon before the dawn. But not for spirit-presences. And not for Jesus, His spirit glowing with that inner fire which makes man forget his body.

The shafts of dawnlight kiss the mountain awake. Another long, hot day begins. But before the mist clears a voice has spoken in the hearts of three men: a voice they will never forget. They have seen enough. No outward voice is needed. Within three hearts is a certainty as strong as steel. God put it there. "This is My beloved Son: hear ye Him." The day has begun. He is with them again—in *their* world. It is time to go back to the plains and face the world's sorrow. But He is not quite the same. A certain preoccupation possesses Him. There is a new line in His face; a grim determination that somehow frightens them. He speaks about His death. They do not understand. "And they were afraid to ask Him about this saying." His face now is set like a flint to go to Jerusalem.

from *His Life and Ours*

Lord Jesus, I know not what awaits me even within an hour. But it can be nothing like what Thou didst bear. Yet give to me also the comfort of spirit-presences, for the angels are not dead. Give me, too, the courage to go on. As I leave this mountain of communion, may I serve God in my fellows as Thou didst, without further thought of self. Let me rejoice if pain and sorrow do not fall upon me. But if they do, grant me Thy patience, Thy courage, Thy joy, Thy trust in God, Thy certainty that "with them that love Him, God co-operates in all things for good." Grant me, dear Lord, light for the next step and be with me, my Friend, my Guide, my Lord, until at last, in the next phase of being, I find that everything in my life had unsuspected **meaning** and significance in a vast purpose of Thy conceiving, vaster than I could ever dream, wherein even evil was made to serve Thee and my poor life made to fit into, and even to further, Thy plan. This for the future. But oh, today, give me cheerfulness, enough courage and a quiet mind. Amen.

Day 8

DAY 8 ROOM I

The Affirmation of the Divine Presence

Lo, GOD is here! Let us adore,
   And own how dreadful is this place!
Let all within us feel His power,
   And silent bow before His face;
Who know His power, His grace who prove,
Serve Him with awe, with reverence love. . . .

As flowers their opening leaves display,
   And glad drink in the solar fire,
So may we catch Thy every ray,
   So may Thy influence us inspire;
Thou Beam of the eternal Beam,
Thou purging Fire, Thou quickening Flame.

GERHARD TERSTEEGEN
(tr. by John Wesley)

Be strong and of a good courage. Be not afraid nor dismayed for the King of Assyria, nor for all the multitude that is with him: for there is a greater *with us* than with him. With him is an arm of flesh, but *with us* is the Lord our God to help us, and to fight our battles. And *the people rested themselves upon the words of Hezekiah*, King of Judah. 2 Chronicles 32 7-8

Jesu, the very thought of Thee
    With sweetness fills my breast;
But sweeter far Thy face to see,
    And in Thy presence rest.

BERNARD OF CLAIRVAUX
(tr. by Edward Caswall)

DAY 8 ROOM 2

Adoration, Praise and Thanksgiving

O GOD, we thank Thee for the world in which Thou
hast placed us, for the universe whose vastness is
revealed in the blue depths of the sky, whose immensities
are lit by shining stars beyond the strength of mind to
follow. We thank Thee for every sacrament of beauty;
for the sweetness of the flowers, the songs of birds, the
solemnity of the stars, the sound of streams and swelling
seas; for far-reaching lands and mighty mountains which
rest and satisfy the soul, the purity of dawn which calls
to holy dedication, the peace of evening which speaks of
everlasting rest. May we not fear to make this world for
a little while our home, since it is Thy creation, and we
ourselves are part of it. Help us humbly to learn its laws
and trust its mighty powers. Through Jesus Christ our
Lord. Amen.

W. E. ORCHARD
The Temple

Confession, Forgiveness and Unloading

JUST AS I am, and waiting not
    To rid my soul of one dark blot,
To Thee, Whose Love can cleanse each spot,
    O Lamb of God, I come!

Just as I am, Thou wilt receive,
Wilt welcome, pardon, cleanse, relieve;
Because Thy promise I believe,
    O Lamb of God, I come!

Just as I am, poor, wretched, blind;
Sight, riches, healing of the mind,
Yea, all I need, in Thee to find,
    O Lamb of God, I come!

CHARLOTTE ELLIOTT

Lord Jesus, let there be reality in my coming. Let not these familiar words fail to awaken my response. If only it could all be as real as Thy physical presence would make it! Strengthen my imagination and deepen my faith that I may be made *sure* of Thy forgiveness and go on with "the burden loosed from off my shoulders."

I saw in my dream that just as Christian came up with the Cross, his burden loosed from off his shoulders, and fell from off his back, and began to tumble, and so continued to do till it came to the mouth of the sepulchre, where it fell in, and *I saw it no more.*

JOHN BUNYAN
Pilgrim's Progress

Positive Affirmation and Reception

I AM BECOMING more and more aware of Thy power of Goodness, which is Life to the Mind and Health to the Body.

M. V. DUNLOP

As I offer this thought to my mind, driving from it all other thoughts, may it seep into the depths of my being like some spiritual antiseptic, cleansing the ferment of all that is foul, so that there is no part of me in which anything contrary to Thy Spirit can develop and grow.

Thy love to me, O God,
Not mine, O Lord, to Thee,
Can rid me of this dark unrest,
And set my spirit free.

Thy grace alone, O God,
To me can pardon speak;
Thy power alone, O Son of God,
Can this sore bondage break.

I bless the Christ of God,
I rest on love divine,
And with unfaltering lip and heart,
I call this Saviour mine.

HORATIUS BONAR

Petition

TEACH US, O Father, to trust Thee with life and with
   death,
And (though this is harder by far)
With the life and the death of those that are dearer to us
   than our life.

Teach us stillness and confident peace
In Thy perfect will,
Deep calm of soul, and content
In what Thou wilt do with these lives Thou hast given.

Teach us to wait and be still,
To rest in Thyself,
To hush this clamorous anxiety,
To lay in Thine arms all this wealth Thou hast given.

Thou lovest these souls that we love
With a love as far surpassing our own
As the glory of noon surpasses the gleam of a candle.

Therefore will we be still,
And trust in Thee.

J. S. HOYLAND

Intercession

FOR ALL who are in despair, and especially drug addicts
   and alcoholics who are frantically seeking ways of
escape, that they may discover what it is from which they

flee and why they flee, and that they may be given insight and courage and a will-power reinforced by the power of God.

Lord God, help me to enter into the feelings of those who crave the relief and solace which drugs and alcohol provide. Let me not despise or condemn them as weaklings fit only for contempt, since I have not walked the dreadful path they tread, nor been consumed with that fierce desire which burns in their flesh and in their minds. Lord, save them.

I pray for the work of "Alcoholics Anonymous" and for all who are helping their fellows in this field. Let my prayer avail to clear the vision and strengthen the will of some poor victim of desire, that, clutching Thy hand, he may be lifted to new self-respect and his feet set on the road to true manhood. For Thy name's sake.

Amen.

Today I lift up my heart in intercession for:

DAY 8 ROOM 7
Meditation

THE SACRED PASSION OF THE REDEEMER

I WATCH, in imagination, His men gathering furtively in that Upper Room, that holy place so full of memories. I hear two of them quarrelling, even on the stairs, as to who should be greatest. I watch the Master take His place at the low table, and then, having said grace, I see Him rise and remove His outer garment and begin to wash His disciples' feet. Then comes the supper and the whispering which ends as Judas shuffles across the room and passes out into the dark night—the dark night of his own soul and the blackest night in history. I listen to the sacred words about the Bread broken and the Wine poured forth. The new covenant in His blood is established.

Then, in imagination, I watch the mournful procession through the silent streets of the city, down into the Kedron Valley and up the opposite slope into the olive orchard. The full moon makes "the little grey leaves" shine like silver and the night breeze makes them whisper their comfort to the Son of Man.

In imagination, I see the torchlight and hear the rough voices of those who look for Him. Judas kisses Him. Peter slashes wildly to defend Him. He is taken by rough hands and all the disciples flee just as I should have done.

Then I watch the farcical trials that go on all night. Annas, then Caiaphas, then Pilate, then Herod, then Pilate again, and all of it ending in a cowardly hand-washing and the weak surrender to the cruel mob and the crafty priests.

Now He is being scourged. I cannot bear to hear the whistle of those lashes through the air and their descent on to that lacerated back. I cover my ears and bow my head. Will no one interrupt the rude horse-play with reed and robe and cruel crown of thorns?

The procession moves off toward Calvary, but He cannot bear any more and stumbles beneath His heavy Cross. At last they nail Him to it and hoist it upright and drop it with a thud into the hole prepared for it. The thud tortures every nerve in hands and feet. I avert my eyes again, for His are too full of agony. Flies settle on His wounds and on His lips and in His eyes and on His bloodstained brow, and there is none to brush them away. No wonder that darkness falls at noonday! The very earth is sick and staggers in her sorrow. The universe shudders at what the hands of mortal man have done to God.

I read again very slowly the words He spoke from the Cross, and I pause after each one that its wonder may sink into my soul.

"Father, forgive them, for they know not what they do."

To the thief: "Today, thou shalt be with Me in Paradise."

"My God, My God, why hast Thou forsaken Me?"

To Mary: "Woman, behold thy son."

To John: "Behold thy Mother."

"I thirst."

"Father, into Thy hands I commend My Spirit."

"It is finished."

So the Master completed the work which, in a body like our own, He came to do. In that doing He not only revealed the character of God, answering by His life and death all the most important questions which man asks about the nature of God, but committing Himself for ever to the task of drawing man into a right relationship with God. This act of dying is a pledge as well as a revelation. No one, still in the flesh, can do more than die. That is his uttermost. Christ's dying is a pledge that *for ever* He will go to the uttermost, using all the new energies which release from the flesh provides, to make man one with God. This is the true at-one-ment and the great hope of mankind.

> My worthless heart to gain,
>   The God of all that breathe
> Was found in fashion as a man,
>   And died a cursèd death.

And can I yet delay
    My little all to give?
To bear my soul from earth away,
    For Jesus to receive?

Nay, but I yield, I yield!
    I can hold out no more,
I sink, by dying love compelled,
    And own Thee conqueror.

CHARLES WESLEY

O my dear Lord, crucified and risen, and even now, in the unseen, pledged to win my poor heart and save me; accept me as Thine own, forgive all that is past, and send me out, humbled to the dust by all Thou art willing to suffer, and yet exalted to the stars by Thine amazing belief in me. May I so remind myself continually of that great, royal, suffering, deathless love that I may be loyal to Thee, my King, and serve Thee faithfully to the end. For Thy dear name's sake. Amen.

Day 9

DAY 9 ROOM I

The Affirmation of the Divine Presence

"THE Eternal God," it is written, "is thy Refuge, and underneath are the Everlasting Arms," "and," said the Quaker, William Penn, "we cannot fall beneath the Arms of God, how low soever it be that we fall. How low soever it be that we fall, they are still underneath us."

Many there be which say of my soul, There is no help for him in God. But Thou, O Lord, art a shield about me; my glory and the lifter up of my head. I cry unto the

Lord with my voice and He answereth me out of His holy hill. I laid me down and slept. I awaked, for the Lord sustaineth me. *Psalm* 3 2-5

The Lord is my light and my salvation; whom shall I fear? The Lord is the strength of my life; of whom shall I be afraid?

In the day of trouble He shall keep me secretly in His pavilion. In the covert of His tent shall He hide me. He shall lift me up upon a rock.

Wait on the Lord: Be strong, and let thine heart take courage; Yea, wait thou on the Lord.

Psalm 27 1. 5. 14

The Lord of hosts is *with us*. The God of Jacob is our Refuge. *Psalm* 46 7. 11

DAY 9 ROOM 2
Adoration, Praise and Thanksgiving

O LIVING GOD, show us how adorable Thou art;
　　Show us Thy beauty, Thy sufficiency, Thy glory;
Reveal unto us, who are so lightly led away by things of time and sense,
Thine own eternal loveliness: that loveliness which now and through eternity
Shall satisfy our souls with divine contentment that can never fade nor fail. *The Splendour of God*

Loving the beauty that I *can* see, and believing it to be only a faint reflection of the glories of the unseen world, I do thank Thee, O my Father, for giving me a heart that can respond to the seen, and a soul that hungers for the unseen splendours.

95

Let me rest in the thought that at the heart of all things Thou dwellest in unutterable beauty, and in infinite love, and, as I bow in adoration and praise, may I so rejoice in what Thou art, that I may lose sight of self and find that fear for self has been overcome by joy in Thee. Amen.

DAY 9 ROOM 3
Confession, Forgiveness and Unloading

O GOD, our Heavenly Father, Who art the Refuge and Strength of all who truly put their trust in Thee, endue us with Thy good spirit, who under the shadow of events look to Thee.

It is not for us to claim anything from Thee as of right. Our own hearts condemn us and Thou art greater than our hearts and knowest all things. Even so, O Lord, look upon us in this hour when we reject and disavow all passions or purposes which Thou canst not approve or bless if we pursue them. O Thou Who in Thy great compassion art ready, if we be truly penitent, to put our iniquities behind Thy back and to lose them in the sea of Thy forgetfulness for ever, lift upon us now the Light of Thy countenance and grant us Thy peace: through Jesus Christ Our Lord. Amen.   s.u.

This is the covenant that I will make with the house of Israel . . . saith the Lord. I will put My law in their inward parts, and in their heart will I write it; and I will be their God and they shall be My people. And they shall teach no more every man his neighbour . . . saying, "Know the Lord": for they shall all know Me, from the least of them unto the greatest of them, saith the Lord. *For I will forgive their iniquity, and their sin will I remember no more.* Thus saith the Lord, which giveth the sun for a light by day, and the ordinances of the moon and of the stars for a light by night, which stirreth up the sea, that the waves thereof roar. The Lord of Hosts is His name.

Jeremiah 31 [33-35]

O God, the power so apparent in the ruling of the heavens and the movements of the sea is the power at my disposal to forgive and restore. Let me receive and accept that precious promise. Amen.

DAY 9 ROOM 4
Positive Affirmation and Reception

I NOW hush my mind and let Thy Spirit flow into my being as the tide flows into some stagnant backwater, cleansing, refreshing, renewing with sparkling, sunlit waters where before was mud and stench and death.

I will be still and take hold of Thy strength,
and be at peace with Thee.

Isaiah 27 [5]

DAY 9 ROOM 5
Petition

LORD, not for light in darkness do we pray,
Not that the veil be lifted from our eyes,
Nor that the slow ascension of our day
Be otherwise.

97

Not for a clearer vision of the things
Whereof the fashioning shall make us great,
Not for remission of the peril and stings
    Of time and fate.

Not for a fuller knowledge of the end
Whereto we travel, bruised yet unafraid,
Nor that the little healing that we lend
    Shall be repaid.

Not these, O Lord. We would not break the bars
Thy wisdom sets about us; we shall climb
Unfetter'd to the secrets of the stars
    In Thy good time.

We do not crave the high perception swift
When to refrain were well, and when fulfil,
Nor yet the understanding strong to sift
    The good from ill.

Not these, O Lord. For these Thou hast revealed,
We know the golden season when to reap
The heavy-fruited treasure of the field,
    The hour to sleep.

Not these. We know the hemlock from the rose,
The pure from stained, the noble from the base,
The tranquil holy light of truth that glows
    On Pity's face.

We know the paths wherein our feet should press,
Across our hearts are written Thy decrees:
Yet now, O Lord, be merciful to bless
    With more than these.

Grant us the will to fashion as we feel,
Grant us the strength to labour as we know,
Grant us the purpose, ribb'd and edg'd with steel,
    To strike the blow.

Knowledge we ask not,—knowledge Thou hast lent,
But, Lord, the will,—there lies our bitter need,
Give us to build above the deep intent
    The deed, the deed.

JOHN DRINKWATER

DAY 9 ROOM 6
Intercession

I LIFT UP my heart, O God, for all ministers of the Gospel, that those who feel successful may lay hold again on the humility of Christ and realise their dependence on Him, and that those who feel failures may lay hold on His patience, and realise that His claim is only on their faithfulness and obedience. Grant that both may care for Christ's opinion more than any opinion of man.

So for all ministers may this day be one of quiet and happy service in His dear name, with neither laziness nor fussy, over-anxious bustling, but fulfilling the demands of their ministry in the order of importance which the values of the kingdom suggest, leaving that which is honestly impossible today until the morrow, without worry or fear of men.

Grant that all ministers of Thy holy Gospel may live in such close communion with Thee that radiant living may win men to seek Thee, and passionate pleading may win men to follow Thee. So may the ministries of all denominations enable Thee to extend Thy glorious kingdom in the hearts of men, and find their unity with one another in serving that one great cause, and dwelling together in Thine all-embracing love. For Jesus Christ's sake. Amen.

Today I lift up my heart in intercession for:

DAY 9 ROOM 7
Meditation

NOW ON the first day of the week cometh Mary Magdalene early, while it was yet dark, unto the tomb, and seeth the stone taken away from the tomb. She runneth therefore, and cometh to Simon Peter, and to the other disciple whom Jesus loved, and saith unto them, "They have taken away the Lord out of the tomb, and we know not where they have laid Him." Peter therefore went forth, and the other disciple, and they went toward the tomb. And they ran both together: and the other disciple outran Peter, and came first to the tomb; and stooping and looking in, he seeth the linen cloths lying; yet entered he not in. Simon Peter therefore also cometh, following him, and entered into the tomb; and he beholdeth the linen cloths lying, and the napkin, that was upon his head, not lying with the linen cloths, but rolled up in a place by itself. Then entered in therefore the other disciple also, which came first to the tomb, and he saw, and believed. For as yet they knew not the scripture, that He must rise again from the dead. So the disciples went away again unto their own home.

But Mary was standing without at the tomb weeping; so, as she wept, she stooped and looked into the tomb; and she beholdeth two angels in white sitting, one at the head, and one at the feet, where the body of Jesus had lain. And they say unto her, "Woman, why weepest thou?" She saith unto them, "Because they have taken away my Lord, and I know not where they have laid Him." When she had thus said, she turned herself back, and beholdeth Jesus standing, and knew not that it was Jesus. Jesus saith unto her, "Woman, why weepest thou? Whom seekest thou?" She, supposing Him to be the gardener, saith unto Him, "Sir, if thou hast borne Him hence, tell me where thou hast laid Him, and I will take Him away." Jesus saith unto her, "Mary." She turneth herself, and saith unto Him in Hebrew, "Rabboni," which is to say, "O my great Master."

St. John 20 [1-16]

Imaginatively we must be there too. We must *feel* the shadows of that early morning "while it was yet dark." It was dark in the hearts of the women. In their thought He was dead. In spite of all He had said, Rome had won. No one had ever survived crucifixion. All they could do was to collect spices and ointments to anoint a dead body (Mark 16 [1]; Luke 23 [56]). Their hearts must have been filled with fear. Not yet had been banished the beliefs in which their minds had been bathed all their lives. The place where the dead were buried was haunted. Evil spirits abounded, especially "while it was still dark." Besides, they trespassed. It was the private garden of

Joseph of Arimathea. And again, who would roll away the stone that sealed the tomb against all comers?

Then came what surely must have been a glorious dawn. That "dark" began to lose its grip. First the hint of dove-coloured light, then the daffodil and green, then the first blush of pink, and then the growing, crimson splendour and the shining gold, and at last, triumphant, convincing, undeniable, the sun itself in all its majestic glory. . . .

We see the dew sparkle on the grass and we see the long shadows on the ground; we hear the rustle of the trees and the dawn chorus of the birds. Mary finds the tomb open, the stone rolled away from its mouth, and a young man in a white robe sitting right inside it (Mark 16 5). Maybe it was young Mark himself. The level sunlight on his white robe gave him the appearance of an angel (Matthew 28 2–7). "Don't be afraid!" he tells the trembling women. "He is not here. He is risen, even as He said. Come and see, and then go and tell." In a sense, that first evangelist after the Resurrection said it all.

Mary and her companions run one race. Peter and John run another one back to the tomb. The way the grave clothes are lying convinces them once and for ever. The body has evaporated and re-formed in some new attenuation of matter—or that which makes a similar impact on the brain—which is beyond us still. If the body had moved, or been moved, the disarrangement of over a hundred pounds' weight of spices would have shouted the fact aloud. But not a fold is out of place. Even the turban is still "wrapped up in a place by itself," still standing on its side where the evanescing head left it, separated from the grave clothes wrapped round the body. Says the fourth gospel in autoptic Greek:

"And they ran both together: and the other disciple outran Peter, and came first to the tomb; and stooping and looking in, he seeth the linen cloths lying; yet entered he not in. Simon Peter therefore also cometh, following him, and entered into the tomb; and he beholdeth the linen cloths lying, and the napkin, that was upon His head, not lying with the linen cloths, but rolled up in a place by itself. Then entered in therefore the other disciple also, which came first to the tomb, and he saw, and believed."

It was the way the grave clothes were lying that convinced them both. As Browning put it, Jesus had "passed through the body and gone."

Mary couldn't "take it," as we say. She wept to think she could not even perform the last offices for the beloved dead, and here was the gardener to tell her that she was trespassing and that this was no place for a respectable woman to be prowling about in the early dawn. She "supposing Him to be the gardener. . . ."

Then He, the Beloved, Who gave Himself away at Emmaus by the way He broke the bread, and gave Himself away to Peter and John by the way He escaped from the grave clothes, gave Himself away to this devoted and adoring woman by His voice. He used her nickname, "Miriam," and no one ever said it like that, save only He. There just could not be any doubt. The cold word "Rabbi" wasn't enough. The word of awe, as well as adoration and utmost reverence, is "Rabboni," "Oh my great Master!"

What a story! "Touch me not," He says. She must not touch Him yet for she is certain already, without using any more of her five senses, and He is preparing her to recognise Him without any senses at all, to join the blessed who know without seeing, or hearing, or touching. It was different for Thomas. He had to have *all* his senses about him before certainty came. "Unless I touch, I will not believe" (*St. John* 20 [24-29]).

But for them all certainty came. All would have said in the end, "My Lord and my God."

And when, my soul, did He die again? When was this gracious presence withdrawn? At what point in history shall we say, "After this no one could ever get near Him again"? Is He not the Ever-Available, the ever-constant Friend, coming not in vision or voice, but in inner serenity and strengthened wills, in tolerant minds and loving hearts? "Lo, I am with you," He pleads, "until the universe is wound up." "Where two or three are gathered and think of Me, their thought draws Me to them." Time cannot hold Him now, nor matter imprison Him. No one can pluck the risen Sun from the sky and bring dark night again. The sunrise cannot be undone. Christ has risen, too, and never can that glorious rising be undone. "Christ Whose glory fills the skies . . . !"

> Whatever clouds may veil the sky,
> Never is night again.

Oh risen and shining One, Victor of Death, there still is darkness in my heart! I sometimes live as though Thou wert dead. In the quietness, as I meditate, dawn upon me and speak my name. Let me become as certain of Thee as did the men and women on that far-off morning.

Mary Magdalene cometh and telleth the disciples, "I have seen the Lord. . . ."

Jesus came and stood in the midst and saith unto them, "Peace be unto you. . . ."

The disciples therefore were glad when they saw the Lord. Jesus therefore said to them again, "Peace be unto you: as the Father hath sent Me, even so send I you."

St. John 20 [18-21]

Dear Master, send me out also, gladdened, convinced and certain, never again to doubt. Amen.

The Affirmation of the Divine Presence

GOD IS OUR Refuge and Strength, a very present help in trouble. Therefore will we not fear. . . .

There is a river, the streams whereof make glad the city of God, the holy place of the tabernacles (tents) of the Most High.

God is in the midst of her; she shall not be moved. God shall help her, and that right early.

The Lord of Hosts is *with us*. The God of Jacob is our Refuge.

Be still, and know that I am God.

The Lord of Hosts is *with us*. The God of Jacob is our Refuge.

Psalm 46 [1, 2, 4, 5, 7, 10, 11]

DAY 10 ROOM 2

Adoration, Praise and Thanksgiving

O LORD, my God, I adore and worship Thee. I ought to say, "Depart from me for I am a sinful man." But I cannot say that for I need Thee so desperately and there is nowhere else to go; no one else to whom to turn who really understands.

So I bow in Thy presence and in imagination I hear the seraphim—in voices awed and rapt and hushed by a solemnity that seems almost tangible, as though the place were filled with smoke—as they cry:

"HOLY, HOLY, HOLY,

is the Lord of Hosts. The whole earth is full of His glory."

Isaiah 6 ³

In this place made holy by Thy presence, with some fire from Thine altar, cleanse me. Grant that *my* iniquity may be taken away and *my* sin purged.

I thank Thee, O my God, for being what Thou eternally art.

> E'en so I love Thee, and will love,
> And in Thy praise will sing;
> Because Thou art my loving God
> And my Eternal King.

FRANCIS XAVIER

DAY 10 ROOM 3

Confession, Forgiveness and Unloading

I BRING my sins to Thee,
  The sins I cannot count,
That all may cleansèd be
  In Thy once-opened Fount.
I bring them, Saviour, all to Thee;
The burden is too great for me.

My heart to Thee I bring,
　The heart I cannot read;
A faithless, wandering thing,
　An evil heart indeed.
I bring it, Saviour, now to Thee,
That fixed and faithful it may be.

To Thee I bring my care,
　The care I cannot flee;
Thou wilt not only share,
　But bear it all for me.
O loving Saviour, now to Thee
I bring the load that wearies me.

I bring my grief to Thee,
　The grief I cannot tell;
No words shall needed be,
　Thou knowest all so well.
I bring the sorrow laid on me,
O suffering Saviour, now to Thee.

My life I bring to Thee,
　I would not be my own;
O Saviour, let me be
　Thine ever, Thine alone.
My heart, my life, my all I bring
To Thee, my Saviour and my King.

FRANCES R. HAVERGAL

Humble yourselves therefore under the mighty hand
of God, that He may exalt you in due time, casting all
your anxiety upon Him, because He careth for you.

1 Peter 5 [6-7]

Cast thy burden upon the Lord, and He shall sustain
thee.　　　　　　　　　　　　　　　Psalm 55 [22]

Positive Affirmation and Reception

THE TRANSFORMING power of God is at work within me.

The trend of Nature is towards completion and perfection. My cut finger *tends* to heal. The scarred earth *tends* to become reclothed in living green. The swallow, trapped and caged, longs to be off as winter draws near, and beats its wings against the bars. Open the cage and at once it sets off for the south. The tops of my garden trees were lopped off. Soon the highest boughs, which were previously horizontal, pointed towards the sky and the shape of the trees began to conform to pattern. There was a *trend* towards beauty. Tired, I lie down and relax, and healing, recuperative energies start at once to make me rested and renewed. There is a "healing power of Nature" at work in body, mind and spirit.

In so many instances there is a trend towards repair, towards beauty, completion, perfection.

Oh, in my soul let me welcome that transforming power, believe in it, foster it, encourage it, and by my faith in its working, release it in greater measure that I, too, may be complete in Thee, my God.

I receive the truth, even as I affirm it: the transforming power of God is at work within me.

Petition

SON OF GOD, if Thy free grace
  Again hath raised me up,
Called me still to seek Thy face,
  And given me back my hope;

Still Thy timely help afford,
And all Thy loving-kindness show:
  Keep me, keep me, gracious Lord,
    And never let me go!

By me, O my Saviour, stand
  In sore temptation's hour;
Save me with Thine outstretched hand,
  And show forth all Thy power;
O be mindful of Thy word,
Thy all-sufficient grace bestow:
  Keep me, keep me, gracious Lord,
    And never let me go!

Give me, Lord, a holy fear,
  And fix it in my heart,
That I may from evil near
  With timely care depart;
Sin be more than hell abhorred;
Till Thou destroy the tyrant foe,
  Keep me, keep me, gracious Lord,
    And never let me go!

Never let me leave Thy breast,
  From Thee, my Saviour, stray;
Thou art my Support and Rest,
  My true and living Way;
My exceeding great Reward,
In heaven above and earth below:
  Keep me, keep me, gracious Lord,
    And never let me go!

CHARLES WESLEY

Intercession

FOR ALL who are depressed by their loneliness, that they may be guided to find satisfying friendships and ways of serving others.

That their loneliness may press them closer to Thy breast, so that its worst bitterness is eased, and ultimate gain may enrich them more than the love and nearness of friends could do.

Today I lift up my heart in intercession for:

Meditation

O HOLY SPIRIT of God, I think of Thee as indwelling all human hearts. It is Thou Who dost inspire the prophets, the psalmists, the true poets, the real musicians and sculptors and artists. It is Thou Who dost lead men to that tremendous moment when they feel the shock of truth, and *possess* the truth to which once they only assented. It is Thou Who dost make men turn away in loathing from sin and its dreary uncleanness. It is Thou Who dost make men *know* that in God is the fulness of the life they seek. It is Thou Who dost fire men and women to do the brave thing. It is Thou Who, like gentle dew on a barren hillside giving sustenance and survival to the drooping violet, canst keep alive the lovely virtues almost shrivelled by the barren life of modern days. Like a glorious wind from the sea sweeping through some stuffy town, invigorating men and bringing them messages from wide places of water and wave, Thou dost remind men of freedom, making them know that imprisonment in this earth-life is only for a time, and that they were born for a wider life than they have ever known. It is Thy light which dawns upon the soul after the darkest night and lightens our darkness.

"Every virtue we possess" is Thine, and "every thought of holiness." Forgive me if I have thought too little about Thee! Yet men will gaze on the glories of the world, see the splendours of dawn and sunset, watch the trembling stars steal into the sky, rest their gaze on mighty mountains that seem to bring strength to the spirit, correct their small perspective by looking upon some far-stretching landscape, or reassure their minds by the secret message of lovely flowers, and never once will they think of their eyes to which they owe all that they see. Their eyes are content if men see.

And Thou, O Holy One, art our eyes, our means of vision, and if we think too little of Thee, we love and live by that which Thou bringest to our knowledge and remembrance. It is through Thee that we see, by Thee that we are brave, because of Thee that we long for God. Is it not written of Thee: "He shall not speak of Himself," and again, "He shall teach you all things. He shall guide you into all the truth," and yet again, "He shall glorify Me, and He shall convince the world"?

As I sit quietly in this room of meditation, come to me, nay, reveal a Presence that never deserts me. Meet my need. Be Thou Fire or Dew. Be Thou Wind or Light to me. All my most worthwhile desires would be realised if but one prayer could fully be answered in my needy heart:

Breathe on me, Breath of God;
Fill me with life anew,
That I may love what Thou dost love,
And do what Thou wouldst do.

Breathe on me, Breath of God,
Until my heart is pure,
Until with Thee I will one will,
To do and to endure.

Breathe on me, Breath of God,
Till I am wholly Thine,
Until this earthly part of me
Glows with Thy fire divine.

Breathe on me, Breath of God;
So shall I never die,
But live with Thee the perfect life
Of Thine eternity.

EDWIN HATCH

Day 11

DAY II ROOM I

Affirmation of the Divine Presence

I HEARD a great voice out of the throne saying, "Behold, the tabernacle of God is with men and He shall dwell *with them*, and they shall be His peoples, and God Himself shall be *with them*, and be their God. . . . He that overcometh shall inherit these things; and I will be his God, and he shall be My son."

Revelation 21 $^{3\ 7}$

What Harry Lee wrote about a human friend, we can think in regard to the Divine Companion:

> What wind brings to the lagging sail,
> Rain to the drooping flower,
> Sweet fire
> And the broken bread
> And song's peace
> To the lonely hour,
> You bring,
> And blithely, to your kind
> You come, and lo!
> The sail is spread,
> The flower dances in the sun,
> The heart leaps heavenward
> Like flame—
> And God is in the broken bread.

DAY II ROOM 2

Adoration, Praise and Thanksgiving

THEREFORE with angels and archangels, and with all the company of heaven we laud and magnify Thy glorious Name: evermore praising Thee, and saying, Holy, Holy, Holy, Lord God of hosts, heaven and earth are full of Thy glory: Glory be to Thee, O Lord most High.   *The Book of Common Prayer*

Grant unto me, O Lord, a sense that I am linked with unseen friends on the other side; that angels and archangels, kindred souls on a higher plane and heavenly guides are not disdainful of, or too remote from, my lowly way. Let me dwell on the thought of the august

destiny to which I am travelling; so august that Thou
Thyself and all the hosts of heaven are involved in the
way I play my part.

I, therefore, praise and adore Thee; I thank Thee
and glorify Thee that Thou hast brought me into being
and linked my life with thine. Amen.

DAY 11 ROOM 3

Confession, Forgiveness and Unloading

No, not despairingly
  Come I to Thee;
No, not distrustingly
  Bend I the knee:
Sin hath gone over me,
Yet is this still my plea:
  Jesus hath died.

Lord, I confess to Thee
  Sadly my sin;
All I am tell I Thee,
  All I have been:
Purge Thou my sin away,
Wash Thou my soul this day;
  Lord, make me clean.

Faithful and just art Thou,
  Forgiving all;
Loving and kind art Thou
  When poor ones call:
Lord, let the cleansing blood,
Blood of the Lamb of God,
  Pass o'er my soul.

Then all is peace and light
  This soul within;
Thus shall I walk with Thee,
  The loved Unseen;
Leaning on Thee, my God,
Guided along the road,
  Nothing between.

HORATIUS BONAR

DAY 11 ROOM 4
Positive Affirmation and Reception

PEACE I leave with you. My peace I give unto you.
  If God will not give, I cannot wrest or snatch
anything from His hand. If He will give, I have only to
take what He offers. I take by affirming His promises as
being fulfilled in the moment of affirmation. Thus, when
He says, "I will pardon thine offences and thy sin I will
remember no more," I accept pardon with wonder and
humility. When He says, "I will give you rest," I say,
"I rest in Thee, dear Lord." When He says, "My peace
I give unto you," I say, "This peace is filling my heart
even as I repeat the word, 'Peace, peace, peace.'" When
He says, "My joy shall be in you and your joy shall be
filled full," I know that my heart is filling with His joy.
And why do I ask Him to be with me when He has
promised to be with me? Does one doubt that a friend
will keep a promise? Does one have to keep reminding
him? The person I have to remind is myself that the
promise has been made to *me*.

So, quietly, let me accept now Thy peace in my
heart.

115

Petition

O GOD, help us truly to want Thee. May our sincerest desire be to be like Christ. May He dominate our wills, inspire our thoughts and permeate our feelings. Help us at last to dethrone self. Kill this hateful selfishness and egotism. Deliver us from a "humility" that parades itself for men's admiration; from doing loving things for others but with a self-congratulation that poisons motive. O God, may we be truly ready to be overlooked and forgotten and even scorned, if only Thou art glorified. Dear Christ, forgive our self-assertion and help us *really* and *truly* to want—more than anything— to be like Thee. Amen.

Intercession

FOR ALL who are poor, hungry and homeless, searching unhappily for food, exposed to bitter weather, uncomforted by the immeasurable blessing of home and fire and food, by warm clothes and a comfortable bed.

For all who minister to the poor and needy, especially for the great Missions of all denominations, the Salvation Army, and the loving ministry of Roman Catholic nuns and monks.

Today, O Lord, I lift up my heart in intercession for:

Meditation

Now there were some present at that very season which told Him of the Galilæans, whose blood Pilate had mingled with their sacrifices. And He answered and said unto them, "Think ye that these Galilæans were sinners above all the Galilæans, because they have suffered these things? I tell you, Nay: but, except ye repent, ye shall all in like manner perish. Or those eighteen, upon whom the tower in Siloam fell, and killed them, think ye that they were offenders above all the men that dwell in Jerusalem? I tell you, Nay: but, except ye repent, ye shall all likewise perish. . . . "

And behold, a woman which had a spirit of infirmity eighteen years; and she was bowed together, and could in no wise lift herself up. And when Jesus saw her, He called her, and said to her, "Woman, thou art loosed from thine infirmity." And He laid His hands upon her: and immediately she was made straight, and glorified God. And the ruler of the synagogue, being moved with indignation because Jesus had healed on the sabbath, answered and said to the multitude, "There are six days in which men ought to work: in them therefore come and be healed, and not on the day of the sabbath." But the Lord answered him and said, "Ye hypocrites, doth not each one of you on the sabbath loose his ox or his ass from the stall, and lead him away to watering? And ought not this woman, being a daughter of Abraham, *whom Satan had bound*, lo, these eighteen years, to have been loosed from this bond on the day of the sabbath?" And as He said these things, all His adversaries were put to shame: and all the multitude rejoiced for all the glorious things that were done by Him.   *St. Luke* 13 [1-5, 11-17]

Poor woman! For years she had only seen the ground; on bright days only the shining, hard cobbles of the street or the dusty tracks outside the town; and on wet days the puddles and the mud. She could not look into the faces even of her friends. Of them she saw feet; only the feet. She was "bowed together and could in no wise lift herself up." What was worse, if she was like her contemporaries, she thought her disability was a punishment of God. Did she torture herself for those eighteen years, saying, "What have I done to deserve this?" Then, like a silver bell came an authoritative voice that said it was the work of Satan. Ah, had she but known that truth, how much easier to bear had been her life, even if the trouble had persisted! But Jesus finished the work to which He had set His hand. "He laid His hands on her and immediately she was made straight and glorified God." She saw the sky and, better still, the face of Christ.

Let me not suppose, O God, that every pain and disease and disability is Thy will or man's fault. Disease and pain are never Thy desire for men, and everywhere the Saviour went, He delivered men and in that deliverance did Thy will. Some things may be my fault, my ignorance, my folly, my sin, my worry and fear and lack of faith. But some are my share of the evil of the world. I receive good that I have not merited. It comes from the goodness, the wisdom, the skill of others. Sometimes I must bear the disabilities that come from belonging to the human family. And Satan is at work seeking to spoil Thy lovely world. Thy book speaks not only of angels, but of devils; of principalities and powers and world rulers of darkness.

Whatever the cause of my ill, help me to vanquish it, to feel that Thou art in partnership with me trying to conquer it, and if it may not yet be utterly defeated, teach me that Thou wilt never let it claim a victory. Thou wilt weave it into THY plan and make it serve THY purposes which are wholly loving and wise, and ultimately omnipotent.

In the meantime, dear Lord, make me cheerful and patient, coming to terms with any suffering which I am called upon to bear, and let Thy joy at the bottom of my heart bubble up into consciousness, so that my witness may be brave and that I do not do a disservice to Thy cause by downcast moods and tearful eyes. Amen.

DAY 12 ROOM 1

The Affirmation of the Divine Presence

FEAR THOU not; for I am *with thee*: be not dismayed for I am thy God. I will strengthen thee; yea, I will help thee, yea, I will uphold thee. . . . I the Lord thy God will hold thy right hand, saying unto thee, Fear not, I will help thee. Fear not, I will help thee, saith the Lord, and thy Redeemer is the Holy One of Israel.

Isaiah 41 [10, 13, 14]

DAY 12 ROOM 2

Adoration, Praise and Thanksgiving

HAVE WE not seen Thy shining garment's hem
Floating at dawn across the golden skies,
Through thin blue veils at noon, bright majesties,
Seen starry hosts delight to gem
The splendour that shall be Thy diadem?

O Immanence,
That knows nor far nor near,
But as the air we breathe
Is with us here,
Our Breath of Life,
O Lord, we worship Thee.

AMY WILSON CARMICHAEL

But let me worship Thee, too, O Lord, when skies are grey and dull, when rain or fog blots out everything save the near, and makes even that seem menacing; when bitter winds howl round the house of life, dismay the spirit, and accentuate its loneliness.

Then, O my God, Thou *art*! Thou dost exist unchanged and art still as near as in the sunshine and the birdsong, the starlight and the dawn. Let me hold to this anchor-thought, even though the body trembles and grows sick with apprehension. Thou art, and art ever the same, very near me, yea within me. Let me so worship and adore and praise Thee that there is no room in my mind for fear. Amen.

It fortifies my soul to know
That though I perish, truth is so;
That, howsoe'er I stray and range,
Whate'er I do, Thou dost not change.
I steadier step when I recall
That, if I slip, Thou dost not fall.

ARTHUR HUGH CLOUGH

Confession, Forgiveness and Unloading

DEPTH of mercy! can there be
Mercy still reserved for me?
Can my God His wrath forbear?
Me, the chief of sinners, spare?

I have long withstood His grace,
Long provoked Him to His face,
Would not hearken to His calls,
Grieved Him by a thousand falls.

Whence to me this waste of love?
Ask my Advocate above!
See the cause in Jesu's face,
Now before the throne of grace.

There for me the Saviour stands;
Shows His wounds and spreads His hands.
God is love; I know, I feel;
Jesus lives, and loves me still.

CHARLES WESLEY

Lord, grant to us true faith and trust in Thee. It is our confession, bitter and humiliating, that we have never trusted Thee as we ought. What some of us used to think was radiant faith was so largely youth, health, success and high spirits. Now, for many of us, these have largely gone and we confess the poverty of our lives and the pressure of their burdens. Forgive our egotism and use our poverty to turn us towards the unsearchable riches of Christ. Help us now to seek to serve Thee more faithfully and forget ourselves in that service. For Jesus Christ's sake. Amen.

Positive Affirmation and Reception

THE *measure* of hurt and evil in what Thou dost allow (not intend) to happen to me is the *measure* of Thy purpose for me in what happens. I, therefore, seek to lift the measure of my faith to that high level. For nothing Thou dost allow to happen to me can have, in itself, the power to defeat me, or even to hinder my soul's true progress. Indeed, like Calvary to Jesus, it can be the means by which I fulfil Thy plan, a plan which *uses* man-invented evil. All that Thou dost allow to happen is allowed only because it can be woven into the pattern Thou art weaving for my blessedness, and the nature of my reaction and the quality of my faith either help or hinder Thee and determine the speed and beauty of Thy weaving. I now, therefore, hereby determine not to allow my reaction to be merely the normal effect of what has happened. For the normal effect of suffering and other forms of evil is depression, resentment, self-pity, rebellion, worry, or even despair. I will gather the materials for my reaction from the treasures of the kingdom of heaven which Thou dost offer me—love and serenity, courage and humility, faith and hope. So *joy* will not be quenched by suffering—even though temporary happiness may be— nor my faith annihilated by evil, even though sometimes that faith may be overclouded. So help me, O God, continually to affirm Thy purposefulness through all that happens, and to receive, for my encouragement, glimpses of an ultimate triumph in which nothing is wasted and everything is seen to be infinitely worth while. Amen.

Petition

GIVE US, O God, the power to go on,
To carry our share of Thy burden through to the
end,
To live all the years of our life
Faithful to the highest we have seen,
With no pandering to the second best,
No leniency to our own lower selves;
No looking backward,
No cowardice. Give us the power to give ourselves,
To break the bread of our lives unto starving humanity;
In humble self-subjection to serve others,
As Thou, O God, does serve Thy world. Amen.

J. S. HOYLAND

Intercession

WE LIFT up our hearts, O Lord, for the dying: for
those who can see the gate into the garden of
deliverance and long to pass through it and find peace.
If they have felt unwanted on earth, may they feel
doubly welcomed as the gate opens. If they are distressed
at leaving dear ones and especially little ones, may they
know that they will be able to help from the other side
and that everlasting arms of purpose and of love enclose
all souls.

So may all fear of death pass away in a sense of wonder
and joy as a new life begins, fairer and more satisfying
than earth could ever show. May the utter contentment
of those who trust LOVE, fill the hearts of all who are
dying and may their souls rest in peace. Amen.

Today I lift up my heart in intercession for:

DAY 12 ROOM 7
Meditation

SOME FOLK as can afford,
So I've heard say,
Set up a sort of cross
Right in the garden way
To mind 'em of the Lord.

But I, when I do see
Thik apple tree
An' stoopin' limb
All spread wi' moss,
I think of Him
And how He talks wi' me.

I think of God
And how he trod
That garden long ago;
He walked, I reckon, to and fro
And then sat down
Upon the groun'
Or some low limb
What suited Him
Such as you see
On many a tree,

And on thik very one
Where I at set o' sun
Do sit and talk wi' He.

And, mornings too, I rise and come
An' sit down where the branch be low;
A bird do sing, a bee do hum,
The flowers in the border blow,
And all my heart's so glad and clear
As pools when mists do disappear:
As pools a-laughing in the light
When mornin' air is swep' an' bright,
As pools what got all Heaven in sight
So's my heart's cheer
When He be near.

He never pushed the garden door,
He left no footmark on the floor;
I never heard 'Un stir nor tread,
And yet His Hand do bless my head,
And when 'tis time for work to start
I takes Him with me in my heart.

And when I die, pray God I see
At very last thik apple tree
An' stoopin' limb,
And think of Him
And all He been to me.

ANNA BUNSTON
Under a Wiltshire Apple Tree

Dear Lord, may I take Thee with me today "in my
heart," do nothing that would grieve Thee, say nothing
that I should be ashamed to say in Thy physical presence,

think nothing that is unworthy, and go nowhere, where I should be ashamed to be found by Thee. Let the thought of Thy real presence with me dominate my life today. Amen.

𝕯𝖆𝖞 13

DAY 13 ROOM I

The Affirmation of the Divine Presence

ALMIGHTY God, Whom the eye cannot behold, and Whom we cannot hear with the hearing of the ear, still let us this day feel Thy Presence and know Thy Love, and being stirred and moved above ourselves, thus be lifted into the knowledge of God and the bearing of His holy way. . . .

GEORGE DAWSON

Speak to Him, thou, for He hears, and Spirit with Spirit
    can meet—
Closer is He than breathing, and nearer than hands and
    feet.

ALFRED, LORD TENNYSON
The Higher Pantheism

Because on the branch that is tapping my pane,
    A sun-wakened, leaf-bud uncurled,
Is bursting its rusty brown sheathing in twain,
    I know there is spring in the world.

Because through the sky-patch whose azure and white
    My window frames all the day long,
A yellow bird dips for an instant of flight,
    I know there is song.

Because even here, in this Mansion of Woe,
  Where creep the dull hours, leaden shod,
Compassion and tenderness aid me, I know
  There is God.

ARTHUR GUITER
In the Hospital

DAY 13 ROOM 2

Adoration, Praise and Thanksgiving

JESU, my Lord, my God, my All,
  Hear, me, blest Saviour, when I call;
Hear me, and from Thy dwelling-place
Pour down the riches of Thy grace:
    Jesu, my Lord, I Thee adore;
    O make me love Thee more and more.

Jesu, what didst Thou find in me,
That Thou hast dealt so lovingly?
How great the joy that Thou hast brought,
So far exceeding hope or thought!
    Jesu, my Lord, I Thee adore;
    O make me love Thee more and more.

Jesu, of Thee shall be my song;
To Thee my heart and soul belong;
All that I have or am is Thine,
And Thou, blest Saviour, Thou art mine:
    Jesu, my Lord, I Thee adore;
    O make me love Thee more and more.

HENRY COLLINS

Confession, Forgiveness and Unloading

DEAR LORD, look with compassion upon me as I make my confession of sin to Thee. I have done what ought never to have been done and I have not done—through fear and cowardice and pride—that which ought at least to have been attempted.

I have said impatient and bitter things, cynical and angry things, cruel and unkind things, even to those I love. I have remained silent when a brave or loving word would have healed a wound and furthered Thy kingdom.

I have given a place in my mind to lustful thoughts, to worry and anxiety about what may never happen, to situations that I can *do* nothing to remedy. I have injured my own fitness for Thy service by negative thoughts. Forgive me! Restore to me now the *joy* of Thy salvation. Let the sunshine of Thy loving presence banish my dark moods. Rescue me from myself.

Help me to act on what I know is Thy will and not react as circumstances try to impose. If I am depressed, help me at least to *say* words of cheer, whatever I feel like. If I feel ill, help me bravely, as far as I may, to put the *feeling* of illness and all self-pity away. Let me act *as though* all were well with me.

Lord Christ, forgive the darkness in me of depressed moods and morbid thoughts and fears for self. O deliver me from imprisonment in myself! Dwell in me and shine through me and lighten my darkness with Thy radiance. For Thy name's sake. Amen.

If in that secret place
Where thou hast cherished it, there yet is lying
Thy dearest bitterness, thy fondest sin,
Though thou hast guarded it with hurt and crying,
Lift now thy face,
Unlock the bolted door and let God in
And lay it in His holy hands to take:

How such an evil gift can please Him so
I do not know,
But, keeping it for wages, He shall make
Thy foul room sweet for thee with blowing wind
(He is so serviceable and so kind)
And set sweet water for thy thirst's distress
Instead of what thou hadst of bitterness;
And He shall bend and spread
Green balsam boughs to make a springing bed
Where thine own thorns pricked in;

Who would not pay away his dearest sin
To let such service in?

MARGARET WIDDEMER
Barter

DAY 13 ROOM 4
Positive Affirmation and Reception

I WILL BE still and learn of Thee, Spirit of Peace
within me.

M. V. DUNLOP

The courage of Jesus is becoming mine.
The patience of Jesus is becoming mine.
The joy of Jesus is becoming mine.
The peace of Jesus is becoming mine.

DAY 13 ROOM 5

Petition

LORD JESUS, I am longing
   From sin to be set free:
To find my deep desiring
Forever fixed on Thee.
All hope I now abandon
Myself to conquer sin;
Invade my willing nature
And come and dwell within.

The passing years oppress me,
My growth in grace so slow:
My wayward, fickle cravings
Have leagued me to the foe;
Myself to self disloyal,
I loathe, yet love my sin:
Now hear my heartfelt pleading
And come and dwell within.

If Thou should'st stand close by me
'Tis more than I deserve;
But, being still outside me,
From virtue yet I swerve.
Come nearer, Lord, than near me,
My succour to begin
Usurp the heart that craves Thee!
O come and dwell within.

W. E. SANGSTER

Intercession

FOR THOSE who dislike, and even dread, their daily work. For those in whom is developing a growing terror that they will be unable to cope with life's daily demands for much longer, who dread each returning morning, particularly the beginning of each new working week.

Grant to them, dear Lord, courage and a quiet mind, that they may live a day at a time; that they may feel *Thy* strength rise up within them and *Thy* friendship sustaining them. Speak to them through the companionship of those who can enhearten them, and tell them that "success" and "failure" are man's words. All that is required by Thee is faithfulness in the hour that now is.

For us the trying. The rest is not our business.

T. S. ELIOT

Grant, we beseech Thee, merciful Lord, to Thy faithful people pardon and peace, that they may be cleansed from all their sins, and serve Thee with a quiet mind. Through Jesus Christ our Lord. Amen.

The Book of Common Prayer

Today I lift up my heart in intercession for:

Meditation

AND BEHOLD, two of them were going that very day to a village named Emmaus, which was threescore furlongs from Jerusalem. And they communed with each other of all these things which had happened. And it came to pass, while they communed and questioned together, that Jesus Himself drew near, and went with them. But their eyes were holden that they should not know Him. And He said unto them, "What communications are these that ye have one with another, as ye walk?" And they stood still, looking sad. And one of them, named Cleopas, answering said unto Him, "Dost Thou alone sojourn in Jerusalem and not know the things which are come to pass there in these days?" And He said unto them, "What things?" And they said unto Him, "The things concerning Jesus of Nazareth, which was a prophet mighty in deed and word before God and all the people: and how the chief priests and our rulers delivered Him up to be condemned to death, and crucified Him. But we hoped that it was He which should redeem Israel. Yea and beside all this, it is now the third day since these things came to pass. Moreover certain women of our company amazed us, having been early at the tomb; and when they found not His body, they came, saying, that they had also seen a vision of angels, which said that He was alive. And certain of them that were with us went to the tomb, and found it even so as the women had said: but Him they saw not." And He said unto them, "O foolish men, and slow of heart to believe in all that the prophets have spoken! Behoved it not the Christ to suffer these things, and to enter into His glory?" And beginning from Moses and from all the prophets, He interpreted to them in all the scriptures the things concerning Himself. And they drew nigh unto the village, whither they were going: and He made as though He would go further. And they constrained Him, saying, "Abide with us: for it is toward evening, and the day is now far spent." And He went in to abide with them. And it came to pass, when He had sat down with them to meat, He took the bread, and blessed it, and brake, and gave to them. And their eyes were opened, and they knew Him; and He vanished out of their sight. And they said one to another, "Was not our heart burning within us, while He spake to us in the way, while He opened to us the scriptures?" And they rose up that very hour, and returned to Jerusalem, and found the eleven gathered together, and them that were with them, saying, "The Lord is risen indeed, and hath appeared to Simon." And they rehearsed the things that happened in the way, and how He was known of them in the breaking of the bread. And as they spake these things, He Himself stood in the midst of them, and saith unto them, "Peace be unto you."

And He led them out until they were over against Bethany: and He lifted up His hands, and blessed them. And it came to pass, while He blessed them, He parted from them, and was carried up into heaven. And they worshipped Him, and returned to Jerusalem with great joy.   *St. Luke 24* [13-36. 50-52]

Two despairing people on the road to Emmaus, Cleopas and his wife, go home from Jerusalem with sad hearts. "We hoped that it was He Who should redeem Israel" (21). Then the Stranger, whose seeming ignorance must have irritated them. "Don't you know what has been happening?" Then the strange, fascinating argument: "He opened to us the scriptures" (32). "Wasn't it just like Him to suffer these things and enter into His glory?" They reach their cottage, and Cleopas asks Him in, but He sees the wife's face fall. These husbands who suddenly ask strangers to supper! Perhaps there is nothing in the pantry. They have been away for days. So, with typical and sensitive courtesy, "He made as though He would go further." But she wanted to hear more, too. They constrained Him. After all, they had bread and olives with them, and some dried fish. And they had good neighbours. She nodded to her husband.

It was the way He broke a piece of bread when He said grace that revealed His identity. "They knew Him by the breaking of the bread." And then He was not there—or was He—or had the word "there" any meaning for Him? Was He not, and is He not, anywhere where loving people want Him? He can be here and there at the same time. Back they went to Jerusalem, late though it was and an eight-mile journey, and then, in that upper room, as they began to tell the others, He was "there," saying, "Peace be unto you." Distance is no difficulty. Space does not matter. Shut doors do not keep Him out. He has gone "out of the here into the everywhere."

Lord Jesus, my Western mind would be frightened by Thine "appearing." But come with the same reality and make me as sure as they were. My faith, too, is dim. Not in vision, nor in voice, but in a mind that is serene, a heart that is filled with joy, and a will that is undaunted, prove that Thou hast been very near to me, even to me. My eyes are holden too, but let my heart be sure. They were so sure that they rejoiced even when they could *see* Thee no longer. Give to my longing heart that certainty and that unending joy. Amen.

The Affirmation of the Divine Presence

JESUS SAID, "Lo, I am *with you* every day until the consummation of the age." *St. Matthew* 28 20

Jesus said, "Where two or three are gathered together in My name, there am I in the midst of them."
St. Matthew 18 20

Jesus said, "He [the Father] shall give you another Comforter, that He may be *with you* for ever."
St. John 14 16

They who tread the path of labour
Follow where My feet have trod;
Those who work without complaining
Do the holy will of God;
Nevermore thou needest seek Me;
I am *with thee* everywhere;
Raise the stone, and thou shalt find Me;
Cleave the wood and I am there. . . .

Every task, however simple,
Sets the soul that does it free:
Every deed of love and mercy
Done to man is done to Me.
Nevermore thou needest seek Me;
I am *with thee* everywhere;
Raise the stone, and thou shalt find Me;
Cleave the wood and I am there.

HENRY VAN DYKE
The Toiling of Felix

I can do my work today in Thy presence, and I can make of it an offering to Thee and a contribution to Thy cause.

Adoration, Praise and Thanksgiving

I THANK Thee, God, that I have lived
  In this great world and known its many joys;
The song of birds, the strong, sweet scent of hay
And cooling breezes in the secret dusk,
The flaming sunsets at the close of day,
Hills, and the lonely, heather-covered moors,
Music at night, and moonlight on the sea,
The beat of waves upon the rocky shore
And wild, white spray, flung high in ecstasy:
The faithful eyes of dogs, and treasured books.
The love of kin and fellowship of friends,
And all that makes life dear and beautiful.
I thank Thee, too, that there has come to me
A little sorrow and, sometimes, defeat,
A little heartache and the loneliness
That comes with parting, and the word, "Goodbye,"
Dawn breaking after dreary hours of pain,
When I discovered that night's gloom *must* yield
And morning light break through to me again.
Because of these and other blessings poured
Unasked upon my wondering head,
Because I know that there is yet to come
An even richer and more glorious life,
And most of all, because Thine only Son
Once sacrificed life's loveliness for me—
I thank Thee, God, that I have lived.

ELIZABETH CRAVEN

Confession, Forgiveness and Unloading

IF WE confess our sins, He is faithful and righteous to forgive us our sins—to re-establish the broken relationship of mutual love as though our sin had never broken it on our side—and to cleanse us—by His endless and patient striving with us—from all unrighteousness. Lord, I confess. Do Thou forgive.

1 *John* 1 [9]

Let me realise that that forgiveness is not just the cancelling of a debt or even the bearing of a burden, still less a "letting off" of all consequence—but the restoration of a relationship so rich and new that I, even I, can lift up my head and look into Thy face and, in spite of all the past, say humbly, even to Thee, in this moment: "There is nothing between us." Amen.

Positive Affirmation and Reception

LET ME assert that whatever has happened to me or will happen to me, Love is the Reality behind the universe and is finally triumphant and victorious.

Let no resentment, bitterness, cynicism, or even doubt, sour my heart against love.

Let Thy love now fill my heart and seep into the inaccessible depths of my mind.

God is LOVE, and is seeking to dwell in me in greater and greater measure.

Petition

O BLESSÈD life! the heart at rest
　　When all without tumultuous seems—
　That trusts a higher will, and deems
That higher will, not mine, the best.

O blessèd life! the mind that sees,
　　Whatever change the years may bring,
　A mercy still in everything,
And shining through all mysteries.

O blessèd life! the soul that soars,
　　When sense of mortal sight is dim,
　Beyond the sense—beyond to Him
Whose love unlocks the heavenly doors.

O blessèd life! heart, mind, and soul,
　　From self-born aims and wishes free,
　In all at one with Deity,
And loyal to the Lord's control.

O life, how blessèd, how divine!
　　High life, the earnest of a higher:
　Saviour, fulfil my deep desire,
And let this blessèd life be mine.

WILLIAM T. MATSON

Calm soul of all things! be it mine
　　To feel amid the city's jar,
That there abides a peace of thine
　　Man did not make and cannot mar!

The will to neither strive nor cry,
    The power to feel with others give!
Calm, calm me more! nor let me die
    Before I have begun to live!

MATTHEW ARNOLD

DAY 14 ROOM 6
Intercession

FOR THOSE who are poor in material things and in friendships, for the lowly who despise themselves and think that others despise them, and for those who feel bewildered and lost.

Thou dost understand, O Lord, for Thou didst feel alone, despised and lost on Calvary.

There is Thy footstool and there rest Thy feet where live
    the poorest, the lowliest, and lost.
When I try to bow to Thee, my obeisance cannot reach
    down to the depth where Thy feet rest among the
    poorest, and lowliest, and lost.
Pride can never approach to where Thou walkest in the
    clothes of the humble among the poorest, and
    lowliest, and lost.
My heart can never find its way to where Thou keepest
    company with the companionless among the poorest,
    the lowliest, and the lost.

RABINDRANATH TAGORE
Gitanjali

But let me so pray, so share, so sympathise and try to understand, that I may serve them in Thy name.

Let me be so awake to social evil and the stifling, cramping influence of the social order upon the souls of men that I may strive to get things altered, until the fabric of our civilisation allows the soul full expression and none shall be poor, or lonely, or lost. Amen.

The Holy Supper is kept indeed,
In whatso we share with another's need;
Not what we give but what we share,
For the gift without the giver is bare;
Who gives himself with his alms feeds three—
Himself, his hungering neighbour, and Me.

JAMES RUSSELL LOWELL
The Vision of Sir Launfal

Jesus said, "Inasmuch as ye did it unto one of these my brethren, even these least, ye did it unto Me."

St. Matthew 25 [40]

Today I lift up my heart in intercession for:

DAY 14 ROOM 7
Meditation

As JESUS passed by from thence, He saw a man, called Matthew, sitting at the place of toll; and He saith unto him, "Follow Me!" And he arose and followed Him.

St. Matthew 9 [9]

If any man would come after Me, let him say "No" to himself and take up his cross and follow Me.

St. Mark 8 [34]

Him that cometh to Me, I will in no wise cast out.

St. John 6 [37]

I can see Matthew busy in his little dock-side shelter collecting the dues from the masters of the ships that called at Capernaum. He had heard Jesus before. Possibly he had stood at the edge of the crowd with some kind of wistful longing in his lonely heart. Attracted, but not won. Drawn, but not committed. After all, he was too old, and besides, what would his friends say? How his enemies would laugh!—and he had plenty of them, as every publican had.

Then a shadow fell across his books. He looked up into a face that shone with love; into eyes that spoke, more eloquently than words, of a belief in him which made him believe in himself.

Immediately he knew he must not miss this moment. This was his moment of destiny. All else must be sacrificed, but not the chance of this moment. He arose and followed Him. It is strange to think that we still read St. Matthew's Gospel because a Customs official did not miss his moment of destiny.

Grant, O Lord, that whenever I read about Matthew, I may resolve once more to follow Thee more closely; that whatever else I may miss in life, I may not miss any chance of serving Thee.

So I am watching quietly every day,
Whenever the sun shines brightly, I rise and say,
"Surely it is the shining of His face," . . .
Whenever a shadow falls across the window of my room
Where I am working my appointed task,
I lift my head, and watch the door, and ask
If He has come.

BARBARA MacANDREW

Coming from *Ezekiel and Other Poems*

Come, in this quiet moment of meditation; call me again, lead me in Thy way for me, let the assurance of Thy friendship take away my fears. Let every shadow make me look up into Thy blessed face. Let me rise up now and follow Thee. Amen.

Day 15

DAY 15 ROOM 1

The Affirmation of the Divine Presence

ALL OUTSIDE is lone field, moon and such peace—
Flowing in, filling up as with a sea
Whereon comes Someone, walks fast on the white,
Jesus Christ's self . . .
To meet me, and calm all things back again.

ROBERT BROWNING

He came and took me by the hand
Up to a red rose tree,
He kept His meaning to Himself,
But gave a rose to me.
I did not pray Him to lay bare
The mystery to me,
Enough the rose was Heaven to smell,
And His own face to see.

RALPH HODGSON

DAY 15 ROOM 2

Adoration, Praise and Thanksgiving

I TURN my thoughts quietly, O God, away from self to Thee. I adore Thee. I praise Thee. I thank Thee. I here turn from this feverish life to think of Thy holiness

142

—Thy love—Thy serenity—Thy joy—Thy mighty purposefulness—Thy wisdom—Thy beauty—Thy truth —Thy final omnipotence. Slowly I murmur these great words about Thee and let their feeling and significance sink into the deep places of my mind.

One who is all unfit to count
   As scholar in Thy school,
Thou of Thy love hast named a friend—
   O kindness wonderful!

So weak am I, O gracious Lord,
   So all unworthy Thee,
That e'en the dust upon Thy feet
   Outweighs me utterly.

Thou dwellest in unshadowed light,
   All sin and shame above—
That Thou shouldst bear our sin and shame,
   How can I tell such love?

Ah, did not He the heavenly throne
   A little thing esteem,
And not unworthy for my sake
   A mortal body deem?

When in His flesh they drove the nails,
   Did He not all endure?
What name is there to fit a life
   So patient and so pure!

So, Love itself in human form,
  For love of me He came;
I cannot look upon His face
  For shame, for bitter shame.

NARAYAN V. TILAK
(tr. by Nicol Macnicol)

Yet, at Thy feet I may bow in adoration and in praise and thanksgiving.

DAY 15 ROOM 3
Confession, Forgiveness and Unloading

BECAUSE I knew not when my life was good
And when there was a light upon my path,
But turned my soul perversely to the dark—
  O Lord, I do repent.

Because I held upon my selfish road,
And left my brother wounded by the way,
And called ambition duty, and pressed on—
  O Lord, I do repent.

Because I spent the strength Thou gavest me,
In struggles which Thou never didst ordain,
And have but dregs of life to offer Thee—
  O Lord, I do repent.

Because I was impatient, would not wait,
But thrust my impious hand across Thy threads,
And marred the pattern drawn out for my life—
  O Lord, I do repent.

Because Thou hast borne with me all this while,
Hast smitten me with love until I weep,
Hast called me, as a mother calls her child—
O Lord, I do repent.

SARAH WILLIAMS

I say unto you, that even so there shall be joy in heaven over one sinner that repenteth, more than over ninety and nine righteous persons who need no repentance.

St. Luke 15 [7]

But repentance must not become a continual brooding over past sin. There should be a definite act of receiving forgiveness, and then we must *go on*, leaving forgiven sins behind us. God does not ask us to live in a state of continual remorse about our past sins, but to OUTGROW THEM and become spiritually adult.

Lord, let me now receive forgiveness, and help me this day to move forward. Amen.

DAY 15 ROOM 4
Positive Affirmation and Reception

I ABIDE realisingly in Thy Presence.
With Thee is the fountain of Light.
The entrance of Thy words giveth Light.

M. V. DUNLOP

Jesus said, "I am the Light of the world. He that followeth Me shall not walk in darkness, but shall have the Light of Life."

145

The darkness is passing away and the true Light already shineth. The Light shines for *me* now. Where Thou beckonest, there the Light shines, and where Thou dwellest, there is peace.

DAY 15 ROOM 5
Petition

FATHER, Who hast told us to listen to Thy voice, give us ears to hear Thy lightest whisper. The daily work and the rush of life around us, and the clamour of our own fears and self concern, make such a noise that it is difficult to be quiet before Thee, and so we lose the sound of Thy voice. Teach us how to be more still. Teach us how to shut our doors around us to all other thoughts, and to make a deep silence in our hearts. Then speak to us, and we shall be strong to hear, strong to do, strong to follow Thee utterly. Through Jesus Christ our Lord. Amen.

Prayers of Health and Healing
(altered)

Lighten our darkness, we beseech Thee, O Lord, and by Thy great mercy defend us from all perils and dangers of this night. For the love of Thine only Son, our Saviour, Jesus Christ. Amen.

The Book of Common Prayer

DAY 15 ROOM 6
Intercession

FOR THE children of our land; especially for those who are unhappy, unwanted or unloved, hungry or cold or frightened or ill.

For those who live in homes made unhappy by quarrels. For the children of divorced parents, children who do not know to whom to give their allegiance or from whom to seek love.

Grant, O Lord, that even as we pray, their angels may comfort them and some means be found by which they are loved and honoured, their conflicts solved and their inner security maintained.

Teach us to remember that the kingdom of heaven is only open to the childlike; that children are the only assets of the future, the only means by which our ideals can survive and our dreams come true. Let us never despise one of these little ones, so precious in Thy sight. Amen.

Today I lift up my heart in intercession for:

DAY 15 ROOM 7
Meditation

AND IT came to pass, as He drew nigh unto Jericho, a certain blind man sat by the wayside begging: and hearing a multitude going by, he inquired what this meant. And they told him, that Jesus of Nazareth passeth by. And he cried, saying, "Jesus, Thou Son of David, have mercy on me." And they that went before rebuked him, that he should hold his peace: but he cried out the more a great deal, "Thou Son of David, have mercy on me." And Jesus stood, and commanded him to be brought unto Him: and when he was come near, He asked him, "What wilt thou that I should do unto thee?" And he said, "Lord, that I may receive my sight." And Jesus said unto him, "Receive thy sight: thy faith hath made thee whole." And immediately he received his sight, and followed Him, glorifying God: and all the people, when they saw it, gave praise unto God.

St. Luke 18 35-43

Only darkness, year after year. No one could make him see. And then came Jesus, "Jesus of Nazareth passeth by." I hear the agony in the cry—"Lord, that I may receive my sight." And at once the man saw the blue sky and green trees and people and the brown, dusty, Jericho road, and—the Master's face.

Lord, how complacently I have treated this wondrous gift of physical sight! I can see the faces of my dear ones, and trees and flowers and mountains and seas; dawn's mystery and sunset's sacrament, moonlight on water and the night sky ablaze with stars. More importantly still, I can see to read. Forgive me. Make me more thankful. End my pitiful grumbling and fretful worry.

Yet I, too, must pray—"Lord, that I may receive my sight."

Let me see the world through Thy compassionate eyes. Let me see my brother's need. Let me see the lovely qualities in difficult and unattractive people. Let me see the sacred personalities of my dear ones and those whom I touch every day and so easily take for granted. Let me view, as persons dear to Thee, the shop girl, the bus conductor, the policeman and postman, the charwoman and the whore; rich man, poor man, beggar-man, thief. All are *persons* dear to Thee and immortal souls within Thy ken. Let me see all children as Thine, especially the unprivileged, and sick and unhappy. Let me see the foreigner as my neighbour and the enemy as Thy child.

Let me see Thy way with the nations and Thy will for the world. Let me detect the marks of Thy purposes and the trend of Thy plan. Let me see that prayer *is* answered, that men *are* guided, that hopes *are* fulfilled. Let me see right through the blinding things that are seen, to the unseen.

Let me see Thy way for me today.
Lord, that I may receive my sight!

Amen.

DAY 16 ROOM I   𝖣𝖺𝗒 16

The Affirmation of the Divine Presence

STILL, STILL with Thee, when purple morning
  breaketh,
  When the bird waketh, and the shadows flee;
Fairer than morning, lovelier than daylight,
  Dawns the sweet consciousness, I am with Thee.

Alone with Thee, amid the mystic shadows,
  The solemn hush of nature newly born;
Alone with Thee in breathless adoration,
  In the calm dew and freshness of the morn.

As in the dawning, o'er the waveless ocean,
  The image of the morning star doth rest;
So in this stillness, Thou beholdest only
  Thine image in the waters of my breast.

149

Still, still with Thee! As to each newborn morning
   A fresh and solemn splendour still is given;
So does this blessèd consciousness, awaking,
   Breathe each day nearness unto Thee and heaven.

When sinks the soul, subdued by toil to slumber,
   Its closing eye looks up to Thee in prayer;
Sweet the repose beneath Thy wings o'ershading,
   But sweeter still, to wake and find Thee there.

So shall it be at last, in that bright morning,
   When the soul waketh, and life's shadows flee;
O in that hour, fairer than daylight dawning,
   Shall rise the glorious thought—I am with Thee!

HARRIET BEECHER STOWE

DAY 16 ROOM 2
Adoration, Praise and Thanksgiving

BLESS THE Lord, O my soul, and all that is within me
   bless His holy name.
Bless the Lord, O my soul, and forget not all His
   benefits:
Who forgiveth all thine iniquities;
Who healeth all thy diseases;
Who redeemeth thy life from destruction;
And crowneth thee with loving kindness and tender
   mercies;
Who satisfieth thy mouth with good things;
So that thy youth is renewed like the eagle. . . .

He hath not dealt with us after our sins,
Nor rewarded us according to our iniquities.
For as the heaven is high above the earth,
So great is His mercy toward them that fear Him.
As far as the east is from the west,
So far hath He removed our transgressions from us.

Like as a father pitieth his children,
So the Lord pitieth them that fear Him.
For He knoweth our frame;
He remembereth that we are dust. . . .

Bless the Lord, all ye His hosts;
Ye ministers of His, that do His pleasure . . .

Bless the Lord, O my soul.   *Psalm* 103

DAY 16 ROOM 3
Confession, Forgiveness and Unloading

OPPRESSED with sin and woe,
A burdened heart I bear;
Opposed by many a mighty foe,
    Yet I will not despair.

With this polluted heart,
    I dare to come to Thee—
Holy and mighty as Thou art—
    For Thou wilt pardon me.

I feel that I am weak,
And prone to every sin;
But Thou, Who giv'st to those who seek,
Wilt give me strength within.

I need not fear my foes;
I need not yield to care;
I need not sink beneath my woes,
For Thou wilt answer prayer.

In my Redeemer's Name,
I give myself to Thee;
And, all unworthy as I am,
My God will cherish me.

ANNE BRONTË

He will forgive and restore for He saith: "Behold my servant, whom I uphold; My chosen in whom My soul delighteth. I have put My spirit upon him. . . . A bruised reed shall He not break, and the smoking flax shall He not quench. . . .

I will bring the blind by a way that they know not; in paths that they know not will I lead them: I will make darkness light before them, and crooked places straight. These things will I do and I will not forsake them. . . . Fear not, for I have redeemed thee; I have called thee by thy name, Thou art Mine. For I am the Lord thy God, the Holy One of Israel, thy Saviour.

Isaiah 42 [1-3, 16]; 43 [1-3]

Remember these things, O Jacob; and Israel, for thou art My servant: I have formed thee; thou art My servant: O Israel, thou shalt not be forgotten of Me. I have blotted out, as a thick cloud, thy transgressions, and, as a cloud, thy sins: return unto Me; for I have redeemed thee. *Isaiah* 44 [21-22]

This forgiveness I now claim, in my Redeemer's name.

DAY 16 ROOM 4
Positive Affirmation and Reception

LET THY heart and mind be single to Love Supreme within thee, and thy whole consciousness shall be filled with the Wisdom, Peace and Health thereof.

M. V. DUNLOP

Let my bearing today, O Lord, carry out and express the affirmation I make of Thy love. Forbid that any grumbling, self-pity or criticism of others should darken the pathway which others have to tread. Let my impact on others be that of light and love, and do Thou, by Thine inflowing love, lighten the darkness within me. Amen.

DAY 16 ROOM 5
Petition

JESUS, Whose lot with us was cast,
Who saw it out, from first to last:
Patient and fearless, tender, true,
Carpenter, vagabond, felon, Jew:
Whose humorous eye took in each phase
Of full rich life this world displays,

Yet evermore kept fast in view
The far-off goal it leads us to:
Who, as your hour neared, did not fail—
The world's fate trembling in the scale—
With your half-hearted band to dine,
And chat across the bread and wine,
Then went out firm to face the end,
Alone, without a single friend:
Who felt—as your last words confessed,
Wrung from a proud, unflinching breast
By hours of dull, ignoble pain—
Your whole life's fight was fought in vain:
Would I could win, and keep, and feel
That heart of love, that spirit of steel.

DR. WILFRED BRINTON
(printed in *The Spectator*)

Peter, the hero of Hugh Walpole's novel, *Fortitude*, said, "It isn't life that matters, but the courage you bring to it." After life had done terrible things to Peter, he heard a voice that said, "Blessed be pain and torment and every torture of the body. Blessed be all loss and the failure of friends and the sacrifice of love. Blessed be all failure and the ruin of every earthly hope. Blessed be all sorrow, hardships and endurances that demand courage. Blessed be these things—for of these things cometh the making of a man." Peter fell to praying, "Make of me a man . . . to be afraid of nothing, to be ready for everything. Love, friendship, success . . . to take it if it comes, to care nothing if these things are not for me. Make me brave. Make me brave."

Intercession

FOR ALL fathers and mothers, for those who have just become parents and have everything to learn, that with loving care, but without fussiness or anxiety, they may deal tenderly and yet strongly with the lives entrusted to them.

For all parents of young children.

For those whose children are growing up that they may be delivered from possessiveness and may accept what cannot be altered or changed; that they, remembering their own youth, may honour and encourage independence of thought and action in their children.

For those who are growing old, for all grandparents: that they may not be interfering or expect a repetition of the methods of earlier days; that they may have humour and patience and understanding and the wisdom to know when advice is wanted and when they should keep silent. Help them to kill within them all bitterness, sarcasm and cynicism and to keep disappointment out of their words and looks, remembering that love is "always patient, always kind."

May all parents realise how wonderfully blest they are ever to have had children and thus to share in Thy creative work in the world. So may they ever turn to Thee, the Father and Creator and Lover of all. Amen.

Today I lift up my heart in intercession for:

Meditation

A LATE LARK twitters from the quiet skies;
And from the west,
Where the sun, his day's work ended,
Lingers as in content,
There falls on the old grey city
An influence luminous and serene,
A shining peace.

The smoke ascends
In a rosy and golden haze. The spires
Shine, and are changed. In the valley
Shadows rise. The lark sings on. The sun,
Closing his benediction,
Sinks, and the darkening air
Thrills with a sense of the triumphing night—
Night with her train of stars
And her great gift of sleep.

So be my passing!
My task accomplished and the long day done,
My wages taken, and in my heart
Some late lark singing,
Let me be gathered to the quiet west,
The sundown splendid and serene,
Death.

W. E. HENLEY
Margaritae Sorori

Love had he found in huts where poor men lie;
His daily teachers had been woods and rills,
The silence that is in the starry sky,
The sleep that is amongst the lonely hills.

WORDSWORTH
Song of the Feast of Brougham Castle

Drop Thy still dews of quietness,
  Till all our strivings cease;
Take from our souls the strain and stress,
And let our ordered lives confess
  The beauty of Thy peace.

JOHN GREENLEAF WHITTIER
The Brewing of Soma

DAY 17 ROOM I
The Affirmation of the Divine Presence

COME IN, O come! The door stands open now;
  I knew Thy voice; Lord Jesus, it was Thou.
The sun has set long since; the storms begin:
'Tis time for Thee, my Saviour; O come in!

I seek no more to alter things, or mend,
Before the coming of so great a Friend:
All were at best unseemly; and 'twere ill,
Beyond all else, to keep Thee waiting still.

Then, as Thou art, all holiness and bliss,
Come in, and see my dwelling as it is;
I bid Thee welcome boldly, in the name
Of Thy great glory and my want and shame.

157

Come, not to find, but make, this troubled heart
A dwelling worthy of Thee as Thou art;
To chase the gloom, the terror, and the sin,
Come, all Thyself, yea come, Lord Jesus, in!

HANDLEY C. G. MOULE

Having affirmed Thy presence, let me live in the strength of that affirmation. Let me not try to manage this day as though Thou, my Lord, wert far away or unable to make any difference to the things I have to face. Come, Lord Jesus, into every experience, with Thy grace and power! Then I shall be courageous and serene and be enabled to mediate Thy presence to others.

DAY 17 ROOM 2
Adoration, Praise and Thanksgiving

O GOD, my Father, I adore and praise and thank Thee because of the splendours Thou hast shown to me. Thou art the Consummate Artist, the Creator of a Beauty before which I stand in awe, and yet in regard to which in some way I feel akin. Without that kinship I should not love Thy beautiful world so much.

I praise Thee for what mighty mountains have done for me, and wooded glades in which the dusk falls like a benediction in some vast cathedral.

I thank Thee for the light on the under-side of a sea-gull's wings and for the joy in my heart as I look up and see him, wings motionless, soaring across the blue sky. I thank Thee for sunsets of breath-taking splendour, and even more for those long, quiet afterglows, when mountains and pine trees have stood out black against the daffodil and green of the evening sky. I thank Thee for certain dawns that have made me feel that there must be eternal joy at the heart of things. I thank Thee for far-stretching moors on which I have picked up tiny, trustful lapwings, until the frantic complaints of mother-birds overhead rebuked my heart and made me put the tiny, fluttering things back on the scrape which, on the vast moor, is the familiarity of home to them. I thank Thee for rushing mountain streams in tiny bluebell glens with shy fish in secret pools, and for many a picnic by those laughing waters. I thank Thee for the sense of Thy power I have felt as I watched waves crashing against the rocks, flinging their spray high in the air. (How foolish it would be to think that evil could win over a God Whose power is glimpsed in Nature's energies!) I thank Thee for the quiet and solemn majesty of the stars, with the unutterable hunger to understand the "why" of Thy great universe which the night sky evokes. For a cluster of primroses in a cleft between grey, lichen-covered stones; for the trill of a lark mounting ever higher into the trackless blue; for the call of the settling curlew, I thank Thee. For the bleat of sheep on a hillside across the valley, and for the crunch of cows' feet on frozen snow as they pass through the gateway of the farmyard on a winter afternoon. For rooks at eventide tumbling into their nests in the elms by an old, grey church tower; for a field of buttercups on a spring morning and a flowering chestnut tree in June; for a moonlit river flowing quietly through a silent night, and for the gentle rustle of silver leaves in midnight trees.

O God of beauty, Who hast allowed me through my senses to catch some faint echoes of Thy nature, accept my tribute of praise. Amen.

Confession, Forgiveness and Unloading

O GOD, THOU art *so* to be trusted and yet we have not really put our trust in Thee. Thou hast *so* guided us in the past and saved us from disaster, and yet we are often so faint-hearted as we face the future. We often walk with trembling, fearful steps, with little joy or confidence. We are so ashamed of our lack of faith, our failure to trust Thee and utterly to commit ourselves to Thee.

Let the memory of Thy faithfulness kindle in us now, courage for today. Help us to put our hand in Thine and commit ourselves to Thee; to ignore our fears since nothing can take us out of Thy care, and Thou art Love and Power.

Forgive us, and be Thou our Strength and Stay, for now into Thy hands we commit our spirits. Amen.

Thus saith the Lord, In an acceptable time have I answered thee, and in a day of salvation have I helped thee: and I will preserve thee. . . .

Sing, O heavens; and be joyful O earth; and break forth into singing, O mountains: for the Lord hath comforted His people, and will have compassion upon His afflicted. *Isaiah* 49 8, 13

Positive Affirmation and Reception

THE WILL of God in me is Health and the will of God shall be done. Similarly the will of God in me is Joy, Peace, Love, Unity, Wisdom, Faith, Holiness and Life. All these potentialities are within me for God dwells within me. One by one I now summon them to consciousness, that they may the more dominate me. I murmur aloud these words, pausing over each one to allow its feeling-tone—not just its meaning—to fall into my mind. I now resolve to *act* in accordance with Health, Joy, Peace, etc. Such action will bring new feelings of Power over the lower self and realisation of the Divine Self within me.

"You see how different this is from the old way of feeling weak and ill and saying, 'This is the will of God, I must have patience and bear it.' As long as we thought that, we were actually creating a state of weakness, because we were really saying, 'The will of God in me is weakness.' Such thoughts as these are blasphemy. . . ."[1] The will of God in me is Holiness, Wholeness, Faith, Health, Peace, Unity, Joy, Love, and Life abounding.

I now repeat these positive words, each of which represents the Nature of God.

DAY 17 ROOM 5
Petition

IF THIS day I should get lost amid the perplexities of life and the rush of many duties, do Thou search me out, gracious Lord, and bring me back into the quiet of Thy presence.

F. B. MEYER

[1] From *The Way of Silence*—Studies in Meditation by Adela M. Curtis, Vol. 5, published by the School of Silence, Kensington, London, 1920.

Let me realise that Thou art the Loving Seeker, and let me not run from Thee and try to hide from Thee in sin or cynicism, in doubt or in despair, in crowding Thee out by work or pleasure, or in indifference to Thee.

Great, seeking Shepherd, find me, and enfold me, for apart from Thee life has no beauty or meaning. Amen.

O Lord seek us, O Lord find us
    In Thy patient care,
Be Thy love before, behind us,
    Round us everywhere.
Lest the god of this world blind us,
    Lest he bait a snare,
Lest he forge a chain to bind us,
    Lest he speak us fair,
Turn not from us, call to mind us,
    Find, embrace us, hear.
Be Thy love before, behind us,
    Round us everywhere.

CHRISTINA ROSSETTI

DAY 17 ROOM 6
Intercession

FOR ALL who are bearing great pain, and who wonder, like lost and bewildered children, why their Father does not come to them, if not to deliver, at least to comfort, and be consciously *there* to sustain them.

For all sufferers for whom the lonely hours pass so very slowly on leaden feet; who wonder in the dawn however they will get through the day, and who all through the endless night, look at the time again and again, wondering whether the dark hours will ever pass; who live for the presence of a dear one, and who, when the door closes behind the departing visitor, wonder why some hours seem so horribly short and others so drearily long, and who weep a little, secretly and silently, because freedom from the bondage of hampering, lonely pain seems so far away; for all such we pray that they may find the courage they need by making the effort to pretend that they possess it, and that their effort may be rewarded by the reality, and by the buoyancy of Thy grace.

For all who feel that God has left them to bear their pain uncomforted and alone, that they may hold on in the dark without despair, and that SOON may come peace, and the soothing and unutterable comfort of Thy Divine Spirit in their hearts. Amen.

Today, I lift up my heart in intercession for:

DAY 17 ROOM 7
Meditation

AND THEY went every man unto his own house: but Jesus went unto the Mount of Olives. And early in the morning He came again into the temple, and all the people came unto Him; and He sat down, and taught them. And the Scribes and the Pharisees bring a woman taken in adultery; and having set her in the midst, they say unto Him, "Master, this woman hath been taken in adultery, in the very act. Now in the law Moses commanded us to stone such: what then sayest Thou of her?" And this they said, tempting Him, that they might have whereof to accuse Him. But Jesus stooped down, and with His finger wrote on the ground. But when they continued asking Him, He lifted up Himself, and said unto them, "He that is without sin among you, let him first cast a stone at her." And again He stooped down and with His finger wrote on the ground. And they, when they heard it, went out one by one, beginning from the eldest, even unto the last: and Jesus was left alone, and the woman, where she was, in the midst. And Jesus lifted up Himself, and said unto her, "Woman, where are they? Did no man condemn thee?" And she said, "No man, Lord." And Jesus said, "Neither do I condemn thee: go thy way; from henceforth sin no more."

St. John 7 [53]–8 [11]

A priceless story, and so like Jesus. It was omitted from many versions, possibly because solemn ecclesiastics thought it implied a light view of adultery, for which the punishment was stoning. Its loving generosity is so wonderful that men were afraid to tell it. Probably the woman was naked. Women caught in adultery were stoned thus. Hence Jesus stoops and fingers the sand. There are enough eyes on her already, many of them lustful and lascivious. He cannot escape, but by stooping and fingering the dust, He can save her the pain of His own pure glance. The Pharisees use her "case" to trap Jesus. What a sublime reply! "Let the man without sin [= without a sinful desire] cast the first stone." No wonder they drifted away, the older sinners first, for age is more afraid than youth of guilt. "Neither do I condemn thee." Not

that He does not condemn adultery, but there is no
need to do so. She condemns herself. His blame would
have swept her away from Him in spirit and made a gulf
between them; it would have rubbed salt in a wound that
hurt badly enough as it was. Note the comfort and healing
of His word, "Go thy way!"

So I bring my sins to Thee, dear Master. My pride,
my lack of faith, my egotism, my . . . It is not Thy word
of condemnation that I dread. It is my judgment of
myself when in Thy presence, a judgment that is so
inevitable, inescapable, remorseless.

Now I bow at Thy feet; I, to whom so much has been
given, resenting trifling setbacks, rebelling against
trivial pain, hurt by justifiable criticism, and I feel so
ashamed.

Raise me up, I pray Thee, and forgive me, and bid
me also, "Go in peace." If only I could "sin no more,"
how deep and real and growing in intensity would that
peace become! Help me, O my Saviour!

DAY 18 ROOM I   **Day 18**

The Affirmation of the Divine Presence

FEAR NOT, for I have redeemed thee; I have called
thee by thy name, thou art Mine. When thou
passest through the waters, I will be *with thee*; and
through the rivers, they shall not overflow thee. . . . For
I am the Lord thy God, the Holy One of Israel, thy
Saviour. . . . Fear not; for I am *with thee*.

Isaiah 43 [1-3, 5]

God does not say, "I will excuse you from the waters; I will show you a short cut by which you may escape the rivers." If He did, what an insurance religion would be, and how men would rush to pay the premium of a spurious piety!

God does say, "In all the experiences through which you have to pass, I shall be there too."

Thus shall even the experiences which cannot be called anything but evil, the experiences I have hated and from which I have shrunk, be woven into a pattern of good and made to serve the purposes of a holy, loving, wise, omnipotent God.

DAY 18 ROOM 2
Adoration, Praise and Thanksgiving

How shall I praise Thee, O my Father, God,
For the deepest things of all,
For the love of God which is in Christ Jesus our Lord,
For the Father heart that loves me and all my brethren
    of mankind,
For the summons to goodness, for the offer of forgiveness,
    for the chance of a new beginning that comes to
    me in Christ?

I do adore Thee, O my Father.   S.U.

Let this day be a new beginning, full of praise and adoration and love.

O Joyful Light, we come, for in Thee only
In trust we seek, and seeking, find a way.
Strength of the tempted, Brother of the lonely,
From out our darkness bringest Thou the day
Lo, having Thee, we lose not one another,
Sundered-united, dying but to birth;
All worlds are one in Thee, O more than Brother,
And one our family in heaven and earth.

So shine in us our little love reproving,
That souls of men may kindle at the flame;
The whole world's hatred, broken by our loving,
Shall bow to love Thine everlasting Name.
Therefore to Thee be praises and thanksgiving,
To Father, Son, and Comforter Divine;
We lift our voice and sing, with all things living
O Light of Life, the Glory that is Thine.

> (adapted from a Greek hymn
> of the fourth century)

DAY 18 ROOM 3
Confession, Forgiveness and Unloading

FORGIVE ME, my Father. When things have gone well
with me I have left Thee out, crowded my days with
work and pleasure and forgotten Thee. I have been so
foolishly proud that I have imagined I could get on
without Thee, so I have lost the sense of Thy dear presence and from my life I have lost those things which
depart with Thee. I was content with human companionship and often scamped or omitted my prayers. Joy and

health, success and comfort, youth and high spirits made me indifferent to Thee, Who didst give them all. Let me in future see *Thee* in all Thy gifts, seek communion with Thee when I feel no need of Thee, and cling to Thee as I cling to a human friend. Take Thy rightful place again, O my Lord, for in Thee alone is life and enduring peace.

DAY 18 ROOM 4
Positive Affirmation and Reception

JESUS SAID, "Courage, it is I." So it must be possible to be courageous. He does not exhort us to impossibilities.[1] One feels it was all right for Peter. He could see the Master's face and hear the ringing tones in which the words were said.

Dear Master, give me now such a sense of Thy presence, such imaginative insight, such sensitiveness to the unseen, that, *as if* I heard and saw Thee, I may receive into my innermost being the impact of Thy courage, driving away my craven fears and making me brave and gay with a gaiety greater than healthy high spirits. Restore to me the *joy* of Thy salvation. For Thy Name's sake. Amen.

I wait in Thy presence affirming again and again, until I really receive Thy assurance—"Courage, it is I "

---

[1] *Matthew* 14²⁷; *Mark* 6⁵⁰. In both gospels the word is translated, "Be of good cheer," but in both the Greek word is a single word ($\theta\alpha\rho\sigma\epsilon\hat{\iota}\tau\epsilon$), which means "courage."

Petition

HELP ME to watch, O Lord, that I do not merely enjoy the reading of beautiful words and call it praying. Make me utterly realist and sincere. Let there be no false exaggeration of facts in order to show myself off in a more favourable light, or win sympathy for myself at cost of another's character or of the truth of things. Let there be no self-pity, no grumbling, no airing of grievances, no recitation of woes or of symptoms merely to get pity for myself. Help me to watch that the traitor-mind within me does not betray me into the constant negativism that spreads depression, creates despair and imprisons me in weakness.

Help me, today, to be positive, to look on the bright side, to succeed in the duty of cheerfulness, to rejoice in the good, the beautiful and the true, and in gratefully looking at Thee, help me to forget myself and consider how best I can serve others.

Just for today, O Master, help me *to try out what I know*, to *make* myself smile; to *force* to my lips the loving and cheerful word, to *experiment* with trust when I feel beaten, and to *act* serenely when all is tempest and chaos within. O Master, Christ, what a small thing it was to cast out devils in Galilee compared with Thy task in my heart when anger and bitterness and self-pity are roused! Come to my heart and bring Thy peace! Amen.

Intercession

FOR THOSE who are unhappy in their work, feeling that their personalities will never find full expression. For those in the wrong job, for all who feel thwarted and for those whose tasks are monotonous and depressing. For those with poetry and music in their hearts who live amid prose and discord. For those who, in holiday mood, never see mountain, moor and ocean. For those who seldom laugh in carefree gaiety and abandon. Show them through some ministry of Thine that they are not forgotten. Show them that they are understood. Let Thy dear Son, Who laboured in a carpenter's shop and yet longed to preach, assure them that one day a Voice will say, "Now God can use you and all you have endured, all you have suffered, all that has seemed denied."

> All that thy child's mistake
> Fancies as lost, I have stored for thee at home.
> Rise, clasp my hand, and come.

Lord God, help all Thy disappointed, puzzled children with unhardened hearts to hold on until they hear that Voice, believing that omnipotent Love will let nothing be lost and that their hour of destiny will surely dawn in this world or the next. Amen.

Today I lift up my heart in intercession for:

Meditation

AND THEY came to the other side of the sea, into the country of the Gerasenes. And when He was come out of the boat, straightway there met Him out of the tombs a man with an unclean spirit, who had his dwelling in the tombs: and no man could any more bind him, no, not with a chain; because that he had been often bound with fetters and chains, and the chains had been rent asunder by him, and the fetters broken in pieces: and no man had strength to tame him. And always, night and day, in the tombs and in the mountains, he was crying out, and cutting himself with stones. And when he saw Jesus from afar, he ran and worshipped Him; and crying out with a loud voice, he saith, "What have I to do with Thee, Jesus, Thou Son of the Most High God? I adjure Thee by God, torment me not." For He said unto him, "Come forth, thou unclean spirit, out of the man." And He asked him, "What is thy name?" And he saith unto Him, "My name is Legion; for we are many." And he besought Him much that He would not send them away out of the country. Now there was there on the mountain-side a great herd of swine feeding. And they besought Him, saying, "Send us into the swine, that we may enter into them." And He gave them leave. And the unclean spirits came out, and entered into the swine: and the herd rushed down the steep into the sea, in number about two thousand; and they were choked in the sea. And they that fed them fled, and told it in the city, and in the country. And they came to see what it was that had come to pass. And they come to Jesus, and behold him that was possessed with devils sitting, clothed and in his right mind, even him that had the legion: and they were afraid. And they that saw it declared unto them how it befell him that was possessed with devils, and concerning the swine. And they began to beseech Him to depart from their borders. And as He was entering into the boat, he that had been possessed with devils besought Him that he might be with Him. And He suffered him not, but saith unto him, "Go to thy house unto thy friends, and tell them how great things the Lord hath done for thee, and how He had mercy on thee." And he went his way, and began to publish in Decapolis how great things Jesus had done for him: and all men did marvel. *St. Mark* 5 $^{1-20}$ ·

I can imagine that steep bluff rising out of the sea: a place of tombs and swine, doubly unclean to the Jew. I can imagine the poor, fear-stricken man, his chains clanking round his limbs, his banishment increasing his sense of horror, anxiety and fear. Whatever his illness would be called today, he was fear-possessed. But he ran to Jesus and Jesus received him, probably spent all night with him (Mark 4 ^{35}) and cast out all his fears. I see the dawn breaking over the mountains and the man sitting in uttermost calm and contentment at the Master's feet. Together they watch the coming of the dawn. Was ever such a radiant dawn as that, or did ever the sun herald such a day of joy instead of terror? The man would like to have remained with Jesus (5 ^{18}), but this was not allowed. Perhaps so newly recovered a patient could not have stood the emotional strain of moving about with Jesus and especially of being pointed out as an exhibit. At any rate, compassion was not cut off (5 ^{19}) and he became a witness. No priest ever had a more authoritative commission! "Tell thy friends how great things the Lord hath done for thee."

Lord Jesus, I, too, am often beset by fears and some of them are without any known adequate basis. I tremble and grow frightened, especially about . . . and . . . . Thou knowest this inner dread which has plagued me so long.

O deliver me! I bring myself with my clanking chains to Thee. As I meditate on this story, come very close to me. Help me to commit myself to Thee utterly. Help me to remedy what can be remedied and to ignore the demons I cannot expel.

A real committal to Thee, every day, come what may, is what I hold back. Let me feel now that even if what I dread most happens, I am still Thy child within Thy care. A readiness to give myself away for Thee is what I need. O my dear Master, how terribly I fail to be Thy trustful, confident, care-free servant!

Let this be the place and the moment of a mighty deliverance that I may lie down tonight as peacefully and trustfully as a little child.

Am I not Thy child and Thou, O God, my Father? Thou Who dost heed the sparrow's fall will not be heedless of a son, even when he falls from trusting Thee.

The Affirmation of the Divine Presence

HERE IS a quiet room,
Pause for a little space,
And in the deepening gloom,
With hands before Thy face,
Pray for God's grace.

Let no unholy thought
Enter thy musing mind,
Things that the world hath wrought,
Unclean, untrue, unkind,
Leave them behind.

Pray for the strength of God,
Strength to obey His plan,
Rise from thy knees less clod
Than when thy prayer began,
More of a man.   .

DONALD COX
*Witness of a Wayfarer to
Talbot House*

As I bow in the quiet room I have made in my heart,
O Lord, let the hush of Thy presence fall upon me. Amen.

DAY 19 ROOM 2
Adoration, Praise and Thanksgiving

HELP ME, O God, as I praise and thank Thee, to do so in advance. I praise Thee, O God, that Thy perfect intention is health of body, peace of mind, and joy of soul for all Thy children. Show me what it is in me which hinders Thee and how to be rid of it, but let me praise Thee in lowly acceptance whatever my condition may be. I thank Thee that Thou art at work within me, that Thou hast not deserted me and will never do so. I give thanks to Thee for Thy healing goodness, not waiting to see its outward manifestations.

I thank Thee that Thou wilt honour the faith and prayer of Thy child. I offer Thee praise and thanksgiving for what will yet come to pass. Glory be to the Father and to the Son and to the Holy Ghost. Amen.

DAY 19 ROOM 3
Confession, Forgiveness and Unloading

FORGIVE ME, dear Lord, for the sins that come to my remembrance when I turn to confession.

I have been slack in prayer and slow to witness.

I have shown resentment at criticism.

I have been irritable and impatient even over trifles.

I have been self-indulgent and allowed words and feelings to get out of control.

I have quarrelled and been slow to "make it up."

I have spread fear through my fearing and depression through my depression.

I have assessed the faults of others as worse than my own without due thought of my privileges and without knowledge of their hard way.

O Thou, before Whom my heart is laid open and bare, forgive me, and help me to do better. Amen.

Let me now accept Thy forgiveness and forgive myself. Let me no longer cling to the picture of myself as unclean, when Thou Thyself, by forgiveness, hast made me clean. Help me not endlessly to condemn and deprecate and despise myself, but to understand myself and move on to spiritual maturity. Let me slip off my shoulders the old filthy rags, and wear, as did the Prodigal, the new, shining raiment of a son. No atonement of mine, no expiation or propitiation is possible or necessary. Thou dost not ask me to atone, but to accept FREEDOM from the burden of guilt, so that the forgiven past becomes an asset in a dedicated future. Let me know now Thy forgiveness and help me from today to move forward. For Thy Name's sake. Amen.

DAY 19 ROOM 4
Positive Affirmation and Reception

I MAY NOW know the deep, illuminating Peace of union with Thee, Most High within me.

I would be healed of all that bears not the likeness of Thy Love and Wisdom, Thy Joy and Beauty.

Healed of all that is unloving, foolish, gloomy or ugly in my emotional life, I shall be truly alive in Peace, for I shall be in the state of fulfilment proper to me as a child of God.

Our failure to meditate regularly, or our acquiescence in negative states of emotion, or our mental subservience to the transient is not simply an obstacle to our own personal development. Our eyes are opened and we discern our negative states as stumbling blocks to others as well as ourselves, something that may hinder them in their pilgrimage to union with the Divine.

M. V. DUNLOP

Remembering this, I affirm and now receive Thy Peace, the deep, illuminating Peace of union with Thee, Most High within me.

Petition

ABIDE IN ME, I pray, and I in Thee;
   From this good hour, O leave me nevermore!
Then shall the discord cease, the wound be healed,
   The life-long bleeding of the soul be o'er.

Abide in me; o'ershadow by Thy love
   Each half-formed purpose and dark thought of sin;
Quench, ere it rise, each selfish, low desire;
   And keep my soul as Thine, calm and divine.

As some rare perfume in a vase of clay
   Pervades it with a fragrance not its own,
So, when Thou dwellest in a mortal soul,
   All heaven's own sweetness seems around it thrown.

Abide in me: there have been moments blest
   When I have heard Thy voice and felt Thy power:
Then evil lost its grasp, and passion, hushed,
   Owned the Divine enchantment of the hour.

These were but seasons beautiful and rare;
   Abide in me, and they shall ever be;
Fulfil at once Thy precept and my prayer:
   Come and abide in me, and I in Thee.

HARRIET BEECHER STOWE

Intercession

FOR THE world-wide Church of Christ in all countries, among all nations, through all denominations, that her essential unity be recognised, her barriers of division increasingly lowered, her power made manifest.

That those who sincerely differ within her may make much of their points of unity and be prepared to act together against all evil.

That all who belong to any branch of Christ's Church may truly love Him, and in Him love one another, that the wounds in the Body of Christ may be healed, and all men rejoice in its beauty, grace and strength. Amen.

Today I lift up my heart in intercession for:

Meditation

IF I stoop
Into a dark, tremendous sea of cloud,
It is but for a time; I press God's lamp
Close to my breast; its splendour, soon or late,
Will pierce the gloom: I shall emerge one day.

ROBERT BROWNING
Paracelsus

Beneath the veriest ash, there hides a spark of soul
Which, quickened by love's breath, may yet pervade the
    whole
O' the grey, and, free again, be fire.

ROBERT BROWNING
Fifine at the Fair

Have we not all, amid life's petty strife
Some pure ideal of a nobler life
That once seemed possible?
Have we not heard the flutter of its wings
And felt it near? It was: and yet
We lost it in the busy jar and fret,
And now live idly in a vain regret.
And yet, our place is kept
And it must wait,
Ready for us to take it, soon or late.
No star is ever lost we once have seen:
We always may be what we might have been.

Since Good, though only thought, has life and breath,
God's life—can always be redeemed from death.
And evil, in its nature is decay,
And any hour can bear it all away:
The hopes, that lost in some far distant seem,
May be the truer life, and this the dream.

A. A. PROCTER

There shall never be one lost good! . . .
All we have willed or hoped or dreamed of good shall
    exist.

ROBERT BROWNING
Abt Vogler

The Affirmation of the Divine Presence

THOU ART, O my God. Let me quietly allow that
thought to sink into my mind. Thou art. And being
Who Thou art, Thou art everywhere. Outside me,
expressing Thyself in every part of the universe. Within
me, working in every cell of my body, and in the thinking,
feeling and willing of my mind. And Thou art Love
and Light and Joy and Peace. So, as I affirm Thy
presence, Thine inwardness, let the thought possess my
mind that every part of my being is pulsating with Thee,
and illumined by Thee. Let my picture of myself—
however I may feel and however dark my past—be that
of one suffused and illumined by the Divine Life. So
Thy Love and Life, Thy Joy and Peace shall become
mine. This is the way of power and health. Thus may I
build up resources for service to others. And when I say,
"Amen," may I sincerely mean,

THAT'S THE WAY IT'S GOING TO BE TODAY [1]

So I affirm and thank Thee, O my God, for Thy
presence and all it can mean to my life. Amen.

DAY 20 ROOM 2

Adoration, Praise and Thanksgiving

MY SONG is love unknown;
My Saviour's love to me;
Love to the loveless shown,
That they might lovely be.

[1] I owe this interpretation of "Amen" to Agnes Sandford's *The
Healing Light* (Arthur James).

O who am I,
    That for my sake,
    My Lord should take
Frail flesh, and die?

He came from His blest throne,
Salvation to bestow:
But men made strange, and none
The longed-for Christ would know.
    But O my Friend!
        My Friend indeed,
        Who at my need
    His life did spend.

Sometimes they strew His way,
And His sweet praises sing;
Resounding all the day,
Hosannas to their King.
    Then: Crucify!
        Is all their breath,
        And for His death
They thirst and cry.

Why, what hath my Lord done?
What makes this rage and spite?
He made the lame to run,
He gave the blind their sight.
    Sweet injuries!
        Yet they at these
        Themselves displease,
    And 'gainst Him rise.

They rise and needs will have
My dear Lord made away;
A murderer they save;
The Prince of life they slay.
  Yet cheerful He
    To suffering goes,
    That He His foes
  From thence might free.

In life, no house, no home
My Lord on earth might have;
In death, no friendly tomb
But what a stranger gave.
  What may I say?
    Heav'n was His home;
    But mine the tomb
  Wherein He lay.

Here might I stay and sing,
No story so divine;
Never was love, dear King,
Never was grief like Thine.
  This is my Friend,
    In whose sweet praise
    I all my days
  Could gladly spend.

SAMUEL CROSSMAN

DAY 20 ROOM 3
Confession, Forgiveness and Unloading

FORGIVE, I pray Thee, O Compassionate One, the grief I have caused Thee by thoughtlessness in impulsive speech and impetuous action. Forgive the unjust judgments I have made and the foolishness of my ignorant declaiming.

Forgive the unheeded fading of earlier ideals, the subtle compromise, the acceptance—all unnoticed—of lower standards, and the dulled and muted whisper of a conscience which once would have cried aloud.

Forgive the pretence of tying a good motive on to a deed when the true motive was selfish desire, and forgive the proud and secret self-interest without which many things, acclaimed as good by others, would never have been carried through.

Idle, and sometimes unkind, words, proud thoughts, unloving deeds, lustful imagining, indifference to needs, selfish motives, all these rise up to shame me in Thy presence.

Let Thy great compassion enfold me and grant me the peace of Thy forgiveness. Make my sin-deadened heart sensitive again, and then give me back Thy joy. For the sake of Jesus Christ, my Redeemer. Amen.

DAY 20 ROOM 4
Positive Affirmation and Reception

THE PSALMIST said to himself, "*Hope* thou in God: for I shall yet praise Him Who is the health of my countenance, and my God."

Psalm 42 [5 and 11]; 43 [5]

There are days when faith falters and affirmations seem unreal. What can be done?

"When the psalmist found it hard to trust, he fell back on *hope* and gained the day. Then he said to himself, 'Leave it all quietly to God, my soul.'"

WILFRID H. BOURNE

So "here's hoping"! And it is a hope founded in God and the experience of a thousand saints.

DAY 20 ROOM 5

Petition

O LORD GOD, since I truly believe that Thy loving, guiding hand is upon my life, help me to be sensitive to every guiding pressure. Let me not make up *my* mind and then ask for Thine approval, but, trying to put selfishness out of the situation, be prepared to go where that directing Hand points. "Where Thou beckonest, there the Light shines." Save me from the exhaustion and frustration of rushing up self-chosen paths from which I have to turn back; perhaps late in the day, when the night is falling. Give me insight that I may see *Thy* way. Give me courage and patient endurance to tread it. Give me faith to believe it will bring me out where *Thou* desirest I should be. And bring me to my journey's end in peace. Through Jesus Christ my Lord. Amen.

Intercession

WE LIFT up our hearts for those who live in unhappy homes; who continue to live together for convention's sake, or for the sake of children, or for convenience or economy, but who find no real joy in one another, who are afraid of one another, who grate continually on one another, getting on one another's nerves.

Grant to them such a joy of heart from *Thee*, born of communion with Thee; such a sense of all that Thou dost bear in loving them; that they, in turn, may be full of a great pity and understanding, full of a *desire* to love and a readiness and tact to avoid the continual bickering and the hostile silences which sometimes come near to hate.

May there be such happiness in Thee that a desire and effort to make others happy over-rides all temptation to be angry or irritable or bad-tempered or morose.

Let the joy of Jesus today banish all the devils of gloom. Amen.

I lift up my heart today in intercession for:

Meditation

LET ME pray for the vision of something beyond the sorrows and sufferings of my life. There are disappointments and disabilities from which I cannot escape, frustrations and failures that are hard to bear. But let me seek to learn what they can do for me, and the use which, by God's grace, I can make of them. Let me gain a glimpse of their meaning and purpose, or, better still, of Him Whose loving purpose they are somehow being made to serve. Then my trouble, whatever it is, will no longer be something I try to get through as easily as I can, but rather something at the heart of which there is a precious secret for me to seek out, a blessing for me to receive. Then will it be indeed a *light affliction*, light in comparison with that *eternal weight of glory*, which, *here* as well as hereafter, it can bring to me. . . .

When I begin to see that realm, that Beyond, my life becomes no longer a purposeless and weary wandering, but a pilgrim's progress, a homeward journey in which I am supported, protected and companioned all the way, and drawn onward by the thought of that which awaits me at the end of the road.

FRANCIS B. JAMES

Day 21   DAY 21 ROOM I

The Affirmation of the Divine Presence

CHRIST, Whose glory fills the skies,
    Christ, the true, the only Light,
Sun of Righteousness, arise,
    Triumph o'er the shades of night;
Day-spring from on high, be near;
Day-star, in my heart appear.

Dark and cheerless is the morn
　Unaccompanied by Thee:
Joyless is the day's return,
　Till Thy mercy's beams I see,
Till Thou inward light impart,
Glad my eyes, and warm my heart.

Visit then this soul of mine;
　Pierce the gloom of sin and grief;
Fill me, Radiancy divine;
　Scatter all my unbelief;
More and more Thyself display,
Shining to the perfect day.

CHARLES WESLEY

Now, in this quietness, I affirm that Presence and rejoice in that bright Radiance.

DAY 21 ROOM 2

Adoration, Praise and Thanksgiving

FOR THE strength of His body and the firmness of His tread,

For the beauty of His spirit and the laughter in His eyes,

For the courage of His heart and the greatness of His deeds,

For the depth of His love and the men it makes anew,

For the strength of His friendship when we dare to trust His love,

For the knowledge of His presence at each turn of the road,

　　We thank Thee, Lord.

GODFREY PAIN

With willing feet I tread the path He leads,
With eager hands I grasp His outstretched arm,
I cannot, dare not, lift my eyes to His,
And yet, I know, with Him I'm safe from harm.

Deep pools of magic fill His loving eyes,
Great joy and triumph, majesty and pain;
If I had strength to let them fall on mine,
Nothing on earth would come between again.

ANON.

DAY 21 ROOM 3

Confession, Forgiveness and Unloading

OUT OF the depths I cry to Thee,
    Lord God, O hear my prayer!
Incline a gracious ear to me,
    And bid me not despair:
If Thou rememberest each misdeed,
If each should have its rightful meed,
    Lord, who shall stand before Thee?

'Tis through Thy love alone we gain
    The pardon of our sin;
The strictest life is but in vain,
    Our works can nothing win;
That none should boast himself of aught,
But own in fear Thy grace hath wrought
    What in him seemeth righteous.

Wherefore my hope is in the Lord,
  My works I count but dust,
I build not there, but on His word,
  And in His goodness trust.
Up to His care myself I yield,
He is my Tower, my Rock, my Shield,
  And for His help I tarry.

And though it linger till the night,
  And round again till morn,
My heart shall ne'er mistrust Thy might,
  Nor count itself forlorn.
Do thus, O ye of Israel's seed,
Ye of the Spirit born indeed,
  Wait for your God's appearing.

Though great our sins and sore our wounds,
  And deep and dark our fall,
His helping mercy hath no bounds,
  His love surpasseth all.
Our trusty loving Shepherd, He
Who shall at last set Israel free
  From all their sin and sorrow.

MARTIN LUTHER
(tr. by Catherine Winkworth)

Positive Affirmation and Reception

I SEE NOW that the loneliness of God is His strength: what would He be if He listened to all your jealous little councils? Well, my loneliness shall be my strength too: it is better to be alone with God. His friendship will not fail me, nor His counsel, nor His love. In His strength I will dare and dare and dare, until I die.

BERNARD SHAW
St. Joan

I affirm that friendship, however lonely I may feel. I claim it. I receive it. Today I will live by it. "His friendship will not fail me, nor His counsel, nor His love."

Petition

LORD GOD, Who reignest over the human body, mind and soul of every individual, as well as over the destiny of galaxies and stars, I can only humbly commit myself to Thee, not understanding the way that I take, its why or its whither, but believing that Thy truest name is Love and that the end of the journey is joy and contentment, the utter satisfaction of my lifelong quest for peace of mind, and the vindication of those values which Thy Son lived and died to establish. Help me, in spite of fears and frailties, and many a coward hour of doubt, to do this. O God of my fathers, Ruler of the whole universe, revealed in Jesus and finally undefeatable, help me really to believe in Thee, and utterly to trust Thee. For Thy dear Son's sake. Amen.

Intercession

O GOD of the nations, I lift up my heart for all who, in our national affairs, are bearing a load of responsibility. In my praying help me to set aside their political views, that with dispassionate sincerity I may pray for them as men and women. In all their ways grant them sincerity and a desire to act in the highest interests of our dear land. And when the burden seems too heavy and weariness overtakes both body and mind, comfort and sustain them and those dear to them, and restore them to serve Thee in all they do, with clearer vision and heightened ideals, that they may help to make our country the instrument of Thy will. Through Jesus Christ our Lord. Amen.

Today I lift up my heart in intercession for:

Meditation

NOW BEFORE the feast of the passover, Jesus knowing that His hour was come that He should depart out of this world unto the Father, having loved His own which were in the world, He loved them unto the end. And during supper, the devil having already put into the heart of Judas Iscariot, Simon's son, to betray Him,

Jesus, knowing that the Father had given all things into His hands, and that He came forth from God, and goeth unto God, riseth from supper, and layeth aside His garments; and He took a towel, and girded Himself. Then He poureth water into the basin, and began to wash the disciples' feet, and to wipe them with the towel wherewith He was girded. So He cometh to Simon Peter. He saith unto Him, "Lord, dost Thou wash my feet?" Jesus answered and said unto him, "What I do thou knowest not now; but thou shalt understand hereafter." Peter saith unto Him, "Thou shalt never wash my feet." Jesus answered him, "If I wash thee not, thou hast no part with Me." Simon Peter saith unto Him, "Lord, not my feet only, but also my hands and my head." Jesus saith to him, "He that is bathed needeth not save to wash his feet, but is clean every whit: and ye are clean, but not all." For He knew him that should betray Him; therefore said He, "Ye are not all clean."

So when He had washed their feet, and taken His garments, and sat down again, He said unto them, "Know ye what I have done to you? Ye call Me, Master, and Lord: and ye say well; for so I am. If I then, the Lord and the Master, have washed your feet, ye also ought to wash one another's feet. For I have given you an example, that ye also should do as I have done to you. . . ."

When Jesus had thus said, He was troubled in the spirit, and testified, and said, "Verily, verily, I say unto you, that one of you shall betray Me." The disciples looked one on another, doubting of whom He spake. There was at the table reclining in Jesus' bosom one of His disciples, whom Jesus loved. Simon Peter therefore beckoneth to him, and saith unto him, "Tell us who it is of whom He speaketh." He leaning back, as he was, on Jesus' breast saith unto Him, "Lord, who is it?" Jesus therefore answereth, "He it is, for whom I shall dip the sop, and give it him." So when He had dipped the sop, He taketh and giveth it to Judas, the son of Simon Iscariot. And after the sop, then entered Satan into him. Jesus therefore saith unto him, "That thou doest, do quickly." Now no man at the table knew for what intent He spake this unto him. For some thought, because Judas had the bag, that Jesus said unto him, "Buy what things we have need of for the feast"; or, that he should give something to the poor. He then having received the sop went out straightway: and it was night.

When therefore he was gone out, Jesus saith, "Now is the Son of man glorified, and God is glorified in Him; and God shall glorify Him in Himself, and straightway shall He glorify Him. Little children, yet a little while I am with you. Ye shall seek Me: and as I said unto the Jews, Whither I go, ye cannot come; so now I say unto you. A new commandment I give unto you, that ye love one another; even as I have loved you, that ye also love one another. By this shall all men know that ye are My disciples, if ye have love one to another."

Simon Peter saith unto Him, "Lord, whither goest Thou?" Jesus answered, "Whither I go, thou canst not follow Me now; but thou shalt follow afterwards." Peter saith unto Him, "Lord, why cannot I follow Thee even now? I will lay down my life for Thee." Jesus answereth, "Wilt thou lay down thy life for Me? Verily, verily, I say unto thee, the cock shall not crow, till thou hast denied Me thrice."   *St. John* 13 [1-15, 21-38]

And when they had sung a hymn, they went out unto the Mount of Olives.

And Jesus saith unto them, "All ye shall be offended

for it is written, I will smite the shepherd, and the sheep shall be scattered abroad. Howbeit, after I am raised up, I will go before you into Galilee." But Peter said unto Him, "Although all shall be offended, yet will not I." And Jesus saith unto him, "Verily I say unto thee, that thou today, even this night, before the cock crow twice, shalt deny Me thrice." But he spake exceeding vehemently, "If I must die with Thee, I will not deny Thee." And in like manner also said they all.

And they come into a place which was named Gethsemane: and He saith unto His disciples, "Sit ye here, while I pray." And He taketh with Him Peter and James and John, and began to be greatly amazed, and sore troubled. And He saith unto them, "My soul is exceeding sorrowful even unto death: abide ye here, and watch." And He went forward a little, and fell on the ground, and prayed that, if it were possible, the hour might pass away from Him. And He said, "Abba, Father, all things are possible unto Thee; remove this cup from Me: howbeit not what I will, but what Thou wilt." And He cometh, and findeth them sleeping, and saith unto Peter, "Simon, sleepest thou? Couldst thou not watch one hour? Watch and pray, that ye enter not into temptation: the spirit indeed is willing, but the flesh is weak." And again He went away, and prayed, saying the same words. And again He came, and found them sleeping, for their eyes were very heavy; and they wist not what to answer Him. And He cometh the third time, and saith unto them, "Sleep on now, and take your rest: it is enough; the hour is come; behold, the Son of man is betrayed into the hands of sinners. Arise, let us be going: behold, he that betrayeth Me is at hand."

St. Mark 14 [26-42]

I see, in imagination, frightened men gathering in an upper room. The Master joins them. I see the flushed faces of the bewildered twelve arguing even on the stairs. I note the Master slipping off His outer robes, calling for water and towel, and washing their feet, and I remember what an Eastern street is like where those feet have walked!

I hear the grace sung and I see the meal begin. I sense the strained atmosphere, pregnant with an unexpressed fear. Then blow follows blow. "One of you will betray Me . . ." and "I must go away." I hear the sandals of Judas shuffle across the floor. A door opens and the night wind stirs the curtains and makes the lamp swing on its chain. Then the door closes. Judas has gone. It is night indeed.

Jesus rises and gives bread and wine to each man. Significant symbols, for it is *broken* bread and *poured out* wine. "These," He says, "*mean* My body and My blood."[1] Only when bread is broken can it be assimilated. Only poured-out wine can be received. They sing a hymn, their voices breaking, their hearts beating wildly.

Then, though it is near midnight, they walk in the moonlight through the silent streets of the city, down past the tomb of Absalom, across the brook Kedron and up the opposite hillside to that quiet, moonlit garden called Gethsemane. I see the grey-green leaves fallen on the orchard grass, the gnarled old trees, and here and there a grey outcrop of rock. I watch the Master move forward from the weary three, who, sheltered by rock from the wind, are asleep at once. The moonlight illumines that stricken face. Great tears and then drops of blood roll down it. Dear God, is this really the only way? "If there is any other possible way," He prays,

[1] See *St. Luke* 22 ¹⁹⁻²⁰ (Moffatt's translation).

"let it not be this way." Even in imagination I can scarcely bear the convulsive throbbing of His breast and the heart-breaking cry—"Nevertheless, not My will, but Thine." At last peace comes. The battle is over. He knew naked terror as I shall never do, but it cannot turn Him from His course. Dear Christ! How can I dare to call myself by Thy name! How can I ever hope to follow Thee? Trifling things appal me and fears beset me and whisper how easy it would be to flee, as Thy disciples fled. I am so often a coward too.

Let the thought of that last night of Thine on earth steady me. I am often amazed and troubled, sorrowful and depressed, but in my case it is often about trifling details. I do not ask for *Thy* courage. Much less would do for me. Grant me enough courage to face each day and grant me that inward peace which comes when the courageous thing is done. Though the heart beats wildly, though the limbs tremble, though the imagination creates terrifying fantasies, and though there is no comfort in any word of man, let me also, in imagination, kneel beneath those embracing, friendly trees, and then rise up and walk in the way of Thy will to find that in Thy will is my inner peace and that all the pathways of Thy purposes lead safely to the breast of God. Amen.

The Affirmation of the Divine Presence

LET HIM walk in the gloom whoso will: peace be
    with him, but whence is his right
To declare that the world is in darkness, because he
    has turned from the light,
Or to seek to o'ershadow my day with the pall of his
    self-chosen night?

"Yea, I know!" cried the true man of old; and whoso'er
    wills it, may know,
"My Redeemer—He liveth!" I seek for a sign of His
    presence, and lo,
As He spake to the light, and it was, so He speaks to
    my soul—and I know!

SOLOMON SOLIS-COHEN

Night does not mean that the light of the sun has
gone out. It only means that the earth has turned away
from it. When the earth just quietly goes on its journey,
thinking, maybe, that it is still turning from the light,
it will come to a dawn more beautiful than noon and
know that the sun never varied or hid its glorious face.

Let me find that I have turned to Thee, O Sun of my
soul Who shinest unchangingly, even when, in my
darkness, I know no brightness and feel that I am
turning away. Make in my heart Thy glorious dawn.
Amen.

Adoration, Praise and Thanksgiving

FAIREST, Lord Jesus,
Ruler of all Nature,
O Thou of God and man the Son;
Thee will I cherish,
Thee will I honour,
Thou, my soul's glory, joy and crown.

Fair are the meadows,
Fairer still the woodlands,
Robed in the beauteous garb of spring;
Jesus is fairer,
Jesus is purer,
Who makes the loving heart to sing.

Fair is the sunshine,
Fairer still the moonlight,
And fair the twinkling starry host;
Jesus is fairer,
Jesus is purer
Than all the angels Heaven can boast.

ANON. (German, 1677,
tr. by Lilian Stevenson)

I thank Thee, O God, for the sight, and even the memory, of the lovely things in Nature: the sound and sight of the lark rising from sunlit meadows on a glorious morning; the dappled light on leaf and branch in a quiet, enchanted wood at noon; the afternoon haze on heather-covered moors that stretch away to the purple distance; the light that comes and goes on distant hills;

the strange peace of evening in a silent valley "when the shadows lengthen and the evening falls"; the surge of deep feeling, akin to worship, when one breasts a hillside and sees a sunset flaming right across the western sky; the hush that falls on the spirit when the scarlet and crimson and gold have gone and given place to the pale-green clearness and the dove-grey cloud. And then the stars stealing into the sky—until the whole heaven and the heaven of heavens are full of their silent, glistening, solemn grandeur. What does it all mean, O God, what does it all mean, unless it be that Thou art utterly beautiful and adorable, and that I, because I love Thy beauty so much, have at least something within me akin to Thyself? Teach me, I pray Thee, ever to link beauty with Thyself, so that whenever beauty touches my nature, I may adore and praise and thank Thee and know that Thou art near. Amen.

DAY 22 ROOM 3
Confession, Forgiveness and Unloading

WILT THOU forgive that sin which I have won
 Others to sin, and made my sin their door?
Wilt Thou forgive that sin which I did shun
 A year or two, but wallowed in a score?
When Thou hast done, Thou hast not done;
 For I have more.

I have a sin of fear, that when I've spun
  My last thread, I shall perish on the shore;
But swear by Thyself that, at my death, Thy Son
  Shall shine as He shines now and heretofore:
And having done that, Thou hast done;
    I fear no more.

JOHN DONNE

DAY 22 ROOM 4
Positive Affirmation and Reception

As the marsh-hen secretly builds on the watery sod,
  Behold I will build me a nest on the greatness of
  God:
I will fly in the greatness of God as the marsh-hen flies,
In the freedom that fills all the space 'twixt the marsh and
  the skies:
By so many roots as the marsh-grass sends in the sod,
I will heartily lay me a-hold on the greatness of God.

SIDNEY LANIER
The Marshes of Glynn

And I smiled to think God's greatness flowed
Around our incompleteness;
Round our restlessness, His rest.

E. B. BROWNING
Rime of the Duchess May

The Bible never makes God's greatness overwhelm us
with a sense of insignificance. "When I consider Thy
heavens . . . what is man?" . . . But it goes on to say,

"Thou hast made him but little lower than God and crowned him with glory and honour." It puts together God's greatness in creation and His great care of men. "Thou tellest the number of the stars; Thou bindest up the broken in heart."

He is *so* great that, unlike the woman "who lived in a shoe and had so many children she didn't know what to do," He careth for me as if I were the only child He had created. I live in Him, and cannot drift beyond His love and care. So today:

"I will heartily lay me a-hold on the greatness of God."

DAY 22 ROOM 5
Petition

IF I have faltered more or less
In my great task of happiness;
If I have moved among my race
And shown no glorious morning face;
If beams from happy human eyes
Have moved me not; if morning skies,
Books and my food, and summer rain
Knocked on my sullen heart in vain;
Lord, Thy most pointed pleasure take
And stab my spirit broad awake;
Or, Lord, if too obdurate I,
Choose Thou, before that spirit die,
A piercing pain, a killing sin,
And to my dead heart run them in!

ROBERT LOUIS STEVENSON
The Celestial Surgeon

Help me, O Lord, so to strive and so to act, that those things which cloud my own way may not darken the path which others have to tread. Give me unselfish courage so that I am ready always to share my bread and wine, and able to hide my hunger and my thirst. Amen.

DAY 22 ROOM 6
Intercession

LOVING FATHER, we lift up to Thee now all who are ill in body or mind; some tossing restlessly in hospital beds, in nursing homes, in their own homes; and others, well in body but sick in mind, especially those in mental hospitals, who seem unable to receive any message of love from their fellows. Visit them all in the silent depths of their own hearts because we lift them up to Thee. If human skill and human faith cannot heal them yet, let them know that men *care*, and, above all, that not one of them is forgotten by Thee. Bring them and us at last to the place where the puzzle of life is made plain and all things are woven into Thy plan. Through Jesus Christ our Lord. Amen.

Today I lift up my heart in intercession for:

Meditation

Dust as we are, the immortal spirit grows
Like harmony in music; there is a dark
Inscrutable workmanship that reconciles
Discordant elements, makes them cling together
In one society. How strange that all
The terrors, pains and early miseries,
Regrets, vexations, lassitudes interfused
Within my mind, should e'er have borne a part,
And that a needful part, in making up
The calm existence that is mine when I
Am worthy of myself! Praise to the end!

WILLIAM WORDSWORTH
(italics mine)

I long for love, Divine and human. Let me meditate
on what it frequently costs. It is not just taking and
rejoicing as one takes the peace of a carefree summer
evening and rejoices in it.

If love should count *you* worthy, and should deign
　　One day to seek your door and be your guest,
　　Pause! ere you draw the bolt and bid him rest,
If in your old content you would remain,
For not alone he enters; in his train
　　Are angels of the mist, the lonely quest
　　Dreams of the unfulfilled and unpossessed,
And sorrow, and Life's immemorial pain.

He wakes desires you never may forget,
  He shows you stars you never saw before.
  He makes you share with him, for evermore,
The burden of the world's divine regret.
How wise you were to open not! and yet,
How poor if you should turn him from the door!

SIDNEY ROYSE LYSAGHT
The Penalty of Love

The pain we have to suffer seems so broad
Set side by side with this life's narrow span,
We need no greater evidence that God
Hath some diviner destiny for Man.

A God would not allow this life to send
Such crushing sorrows as pursue us here,
Unless beyond this fleeting journey's end
Our chastened spirits found another sphere.

So small this world; so vast its agonies!
A fuller life is needed to adjust
These ill-proportioned, wide discrepancies
Between the spirit and its frame of dust.

So when my soul writhes in some aching grief,
And all my heart-strings tremble at the strain,
My reason lends new courage to belief,
And hidden purposes at last seem plain.

ELLA WHEELER WILCOX
Belief

Since it is incredible that God is indifferent to, or defeated by, the suffering of man, then the measure of that suffering must be the measure of His purpose in it and must be the measure of our faith in Him.

The Affirmation of the Divine Presence

WHEREWITH shall I come before the Lord and bow myself before the high God? Shall I come before Him with burnt offerings, with calves of a year old? Will the Lord be pleased with thousands of rams, or with ten thousands of rivers of oil? Shall I give my first-born for my transgression, the fruit of my body for the sin of my soul?

He hath shewed thee, O man, what is good; and what doth the Lord require of thee, but to do justly and to love mercy, and *to walk humbly with thy God*?

Micah 6 [6-8]

This sanctuary of my soul
Unwitting I keep white and whole,
Unlatched and lit, if Thou shouldst care
To enter or to tarry there.

With parted lips and outstretched hands
And listening ears, Thy servant stands,
Call Thou early, call Thou late,
To Thy great service dedicate.

CHARLES HAMILTON SORLEY
Expectans Expectavi

205

Adoration, Praise and Thanksgiving

H<small>OW SHALL</small> I sing that majesty
　　Which angels do admire?
Let dust in dust and silence lie;
　　Sing, sing, ye heavenly choir.
Thousands of thousands stand around
　　Thy throne, O God most high;
Ten thousand times ten thousand sound
　　Thy praise; but who am I?

Thy brightness unto them appears;
　　Whilst I Thy footsteps trace
A sound of God comes to my ears,
　　But they behold Thy face.
They sing because Thou art their Sun;
　　Lord, send a beam on me;
For where heaven is but once begun
　　There alleluias be.

Enlighten with faith's light my heart,
　　Inflame it with love's fire;
Then shall I sing and bear a part
　　With that celestial choir.
I shall, I fear, be dark and cold,
　　With all my fire and light;
Yet when Thou dost accept their gold,
　　Lord, treasure up my mite.

How great a being, Lord, is Thine,
  Which doth all beings keep!
Thy knowledge is the only line
  To sound so vast a deep.
Thou art a sea without a shore,
  A sun without a sphere;
Thy time is now and evermore,
  Thy place is everywhere.

JOHN MASON

DAY 23 ROOM 3
Confession, Forgiveness and Unloading

LORD GOD, Who lovest equally all Thy children and Whose love is as impartial as falling rain or rising sun, forgive my mean, unworthy hates and dislikes.

Forgive me especially for my resentment against . . . and . . .. And as I look to Thee and ask for pardon for myself, I know I cannot have it while I refuse to forgive another. Help me to pray sincerely for those who upset me, whom sometimes I come near to hating, and give me such a keen sense of Thy mercy to *me*; such a sense of wonder that Thou dost not reject *me*, that what others have done to me falls into insignificance compared with the way I have often treated Thee and others of Thy children.

Our Father, Who art in heaven, hallowed be Thy name. Thy kingdom come, Thy will be done on earth as it is in heaven. Give us this day our daily bread and forgive us our trespasses *as we forgive them that trespass against us*. And lead us not into temptation, but deliver us from evil. For thine is the kingdom, the power and the glory, for ever and ever. Amen.

If ye forgive not men their trespasses, neither will My Father in heaven forgive your trespasses. (Matthew 6 [16])

If thou art offering thy gift at the altar, and there rememberest that thy brother hath aught against thee, leave there thy gift before the altar. . . . FIRST be reconciled to thy brother, and then come and offer thy gift. (Matthew 5 [23])

Help me, O Christ, Whose heart never harboured malice, resentment or hatred, to put first things first that I may earnestly repent and being "in love and charity with all men," may find Thy pardoning grace bathing my spirit in a healing peace. Amen.

DAY 23 ROOM 4
Positive Affirmation and Reception

O MIGHTY GOD, Who art immanent as well as transcendent; Thou Who art at work in the distant star, but equally in every cell of my body and every impulse of my mind and spirit, let me affirm that Thou art *purposefully* working.

Throughout my whole being, body, mind and spirit, Thou art striving to overcome all that is at variance with Thy wise and holy purposes.

Let me accept and affirm with thanksgiving Thy victory. I thank Thee that Thou wilt win, and I pledge myself to co-operate and to receive.

Let no negative thoughts or doubts about the outcome hinder Thy work or bar Thy royal progress, O King of my life and Ruler of all nature.

I affirm. I accept. I rejoice. I receive. I praise Thy holy Name. Amen.

Petition

THESE are the gifts I ask
Of Thee, Spirit serene:
Strength for the daily task,
Courage to face the road,
Good cheer to help me bear the traveller's load,
And, for the hours that come between,
An inward joy in all things heard and seen.

These are the sins I fain
Would have Thee take away:
Malice, and cold disdain,
Hot anger, sullen hate,
Scorn of the lowly, envy of the great,
And discontent that casts a shadow grey
On all the brightness of the common day.

HENRY VAN DYKE

DAY 23 ROOM 6

Intercession

I PRAY TODAY for all those who, in this and other
lands, are turning towards Thee.

In other lands many must fear that the old gods will
wreak vengeance on them. They are parting with old,
familiar ways, and in many cases outraging and even
cutting themselves off from those who are dear to them.
Lord Jesus, draw very near to them and make it up to
them. Make this great change seem worth while.

In this land some are turning to Thee who live in homes where others are indifferent or hostile to Thee, and some are young and shy and afraid to show their allegiance, though in their hearts they love Thee.

Lord Jesus, wherever men and women are turning to Thee, show them that Thou goest all the way to meet them, that their reward is a new quality of life with Thee and that Thou knowest the way that they take. Amen.

Today I lift up my heart in intercession for:

DAY 23 ROOM 7
Meditation

NOW THERE was a man of the Pharisees, named Nicodemus, a ruler of the Jews: the same came unto Him by night, and said to Him, "Rabbi, we know that Thou art a teacher come from God: for no man can do these signs that Thou doest, except God be with him." Jesus answered and said unto him, "Verily, verily, I say unto thee, Except a man be born anew, he cannot see the kingdom of God." Nicodemus saith unto Him,

"How can a man be born when he is old? Can he enter a second time into his mother's womb, and be born?" Jesus answered, "Verily, verily, I say unto thee, Except a man be born of water and the Spirit, he cannot enter into the kingdom of God. That which is born of the flesh is flesh; and that which is born of the Spirit is spirit. Marvel not that I said unto thee, Ye must be born anew. The wind bloweth where it listeth, and thou hearest the voice thereof, but knowest not whence it cometh, and whither it goeth: so is every one that is born of the Spirit."

St. John 3 1-8

In imagination, I see Jesus in an upper room reclining with Nicodemus at supper. Some Easterners hate to be overlooked when eating. So I imagine the shutters closed. The room gets hot and stifling, however. In imagination, I hear the evening breeze whispering in the grape-vine that climbs up the trellis fixed to the outer walls of the house. Jesus is telling Nicodemus about the New Birth.

The meal closes and Jesus says, "The wind bloweth where it listeth, and thou hearest the sound thereof and cannot tell whence it cometh or whither it goeth." Then, as He moves towards the shutters and flings them open, I hear Him say, "So is he that is born of the Spirit." The action of flinging wide the shutters seems to make sense of the word "so," for the fresh evening breeze sweeps in, driving away the stifling atmosphere and replacing it with fresh air. The curtains shiver and the wind floats on through one room after another—for this is the house of a rich man—*wherever a door is open to admit and receive it.*

O Spirit of God, cleansing, refreshing, renewing, drive out my stifling fears with Thy health-giving presence.

Let me make sure that all the doors of my life are open to Thee—my family life, my sex life, my church relationships, my business and financial affairs. Let no stuffy pride remain. Let no unwholesome thoughts lurk in the corners of my mind. Let me not turn back and gloat over sins forsworn and forgiven.

> Breathe on me, Breath of God;
> Fill me with life anew,
> That I may love what Thou dost love,
> And do what Thou wouldst do.
>
> Breathe on me, Breath of God,
> Till I am wholly Thine,
> Until this earthly part of me
> Glows with Thy fire divine.

EDWIN HATCH

Day 24

DAY 24 ROOM I

The Affirmation of the Divine Presence

JESUS SAID, "Him that cometh to Me, I will in no wise cast out."

Jesus said, "Come unto Me all ye that labour and are heavy-laden, and I will give you rest."

Jesus said, "Lo, I am with you all the days until the consummation of the age."

I affirm Thy gracious presence. I claim Thy loving promise. I bow in worship at Thy feet.

And Him evermore we behold
Walking in Galilee,
Through the waving cornfields' gold,
By hamlet and wood and wold,
By the side of the marvellous sea.
He touches the sightless eyes,
Before Him the demons flee.
To the dead He sayeth, "Arise,"
To the living, "Follow Me."
And His voice still soundeth on
From centuries that have gone
To the centuries that shall be.

HENRY WADSWORTH LONGFELLOW

DAY 24 ROOM 2

Adoration, Praise and Thanksgiving

LORD GOD, let me now praise and thank Thee for the way Thou hast led me. Many have been my sins. Innumerable have been my mistakes. Often I think, "If only I had my life to live over again with the knowledge I have now." Yet I know that there is no help for me in such idle speculation.

Help me to go forward with a real sense of forgiveness and with a trust in Thy mercy and Thy power to use even my regretted mistakes and forgiven sins as qualifications to help others. Lord, let my future days be a tribute of praise to Thee.

Let me not—even if I am tempted to feel that my powers are insignificant or waning—despair of being used by Thee. For eternity lies before me and death is only a horizon beyond which lies the dawn.

His love in times past, forbids me to think
He'll leave me at last in trouble to sink.
While each Ebenezer I have in review
Confirms His good pleasure to help me quite through.[1]

JOHN NEWTON

DAY 24 ROOM 3
Confession, Forgiveness and Unloading

NO GOOD word, or work, or thought
    Bring I to gain Thy grace;
Pardon I accept unbought,
    Thine offer I embrace,
Coming, as at first I came,
    To take, and not bestow on Thee;
Friend of sinners, spotless Lamb,
    Thy blood was shed for me.

CHARLES WESLEY

So I would learn not to be discouraged when old
temptations that I thought done with for ever revive
within me, when old failures, even, are repeated. I
would come back again and again to my pardoning God
and mighty Saviour, "coming as at first I came." And
yet not quite as at first. With perhaps an even deeper
sense of my own helplessness and need, yet with a growing realisation that I am held in the grip of infinite
Love—that though my grasp of Him is so uncertain He

---

[1] "The men of Israel went out of Mizpah and pursued the Philis-
tines and smote them. . . . Then Samuel took a stone and set it
between Mizpah and Shen and called the name of it Ebenezer,
saying, 'Hitherto hath the Lord helped us.' " (1 *Samuel* 7 [12]). The
word "Ebenezer" means "the stone of help."

will never lose hold of me. He will keep me to the end. Only let me remember this, that in those other words that were so often on the lips of Alexander Whyte, "The final perseverance of the saints is made up of ever new beginnings."

FRANCIS B. JAMES

DAY 24 ROOM 4
Positive Affirmation

My MIND is happy today in the thought that I am God's child in God's world to do God's work within God's will.

This is to be a day of joy and optimism and courage; a day of positive thinking. From all negative thoughts my mind resolutely turns away.

The Spirit of God is working in my body to bring health, and in my mind to bring serenity, and I am one with that Spirit. I am not apart from, or disapproved of, or turned away by, God. No impostor-fears shall let me think I am.

I affirm the reality of health and peace and love within me because God dwells therein.

DAY 24 ROOM 5
Petition

Grant, O Thou Creator and Lover of Perfection, that Thy Holy Spirit may so flow through my mind and body now that all imperfection may disappear and that I may know that perfection of physical, mental and spiritual health which is Thy will for all Thy creation. I thank Thee that now, as I pray, Thy healing Spirit is at work within me.

May Thy Spirit's radiance so fill and overflow my being that the lives of others may be cheered and blessed by every contact I make this day. Amen.

DAY 24 ROOM 6
Intercession

FOR BUSINESS MEN. Our life together depends on them. Our good name among the nations depends very much on their reliability and integrity. The level of our ethical standards depends largely on their honesty and the worth of their pledged promises. Our spiritual life to a large extent depends on their freedom from absorption in the material interests to which they are compelled to devote so much time and attention and sustained effort, often at the cost of great strain.

So we pray for their health of body, mind and spirit, for their freedom from all obsession with material wealth, for a tenacious grasp of Christian principles.

We pray that in a competitive society they may never stoop to what is dishonest, mean or underhand, that they may have the spirit of real service to the community with no compromise with double-dealing or any form of falsity, that they may deal as fairly with their customers as the Master did at Nazareth when He sold ploughs and yokes, window frames and tables.

We pray that thus the quiet peace of their declining years may not be disturbed by memories of wealth achieved by ways they hate to remember, or by any exploitation of the poor or foolish.

Today I lift up my heart in intercession for:

DAY 24 ROOM 7
Meditation

I HAVE KNOWN what the enjoyments and advantages of this life are, and what the more refined pleasures which learning and intellectual power can bestow; and with all the experience that more than threescore years can give, I now, on the eve of my departure, declare to you . . . that health is a great blessing, competence obtained by honourable industry a great blessing, and a great blessing it is to have kind, faithful, and loving friends and relatives; but that the greatest of all blessings, as it is the most ennobling of all privileges, is to be indeed a Christian. But I have been likewise through a large portion of my later life a sufferer sorely afflicted with bodily pains, languors, and manifold infirmities; and for the last three or four years have, with few and brief intervals, been confined to a sickroom, and at this moment in great weakness and heaviness write from a sick-bed, hopeless of a recovery, yet without prospect of a speedy removal; and I, thus on the very brink of the grave, solemnly bear witness to you that the Almighty Redeemer, most gracious in His promises to them that truly seek Him, is faithful to perform what He hath promised, and has preserved under all my pains and infirmities, the inward peace that passeth all understanding, with the supporting assurance of a reconciled God, Who will not withdraw His Spirit from me in the conflict, and in His own time will deliver me from the Evil One!

SAMUEL TAYLOR COLERIDGE
(13th July, 1834, twelve days before his death)
(from *A Diary of Readings*, J. Baillie)

The tree
That fell last year
Knows now just why it fell;
   Why came that hell
Of axe and saw, and leaping, clear blue flame.
   To the world's uses it was set
In pit, or ship, or polished cabinet,
   Or other needs of man.
   The spirit of the tree
   Knows now the plan
   Of that, its agony.

So we,
Fall'n in the mire,
Shall some day surely know
   Why life held blow
On blow, and sacrificial fire and knife;
Seeing one stand the firmer for our rout,
Or some brave, laughing ship of youth sail out
The braver for our pain.
   So—knowing, seeing—we
   Shall smile again
   At this our Calvary.

CONSTANCE HOLM

The Affirmation of the Divine Presence

Go NOT, my soul, in search of Him,
  Thou wilt not find Him there,
Or in the depths of shadow dim,
  Or heights of upper air.

For not in far-off realms of space
  The Spirit hath His throne;
In every heart He findeth place,
  And waiteth to be known.

Thou shalt not want for company,
  Nor pitch thy tent alone;
Th' indwelling God will go *with thee*,
  And show thee of His own.

O gift of gifts, O grace of grace,
  That God should condescend
To make thy heart His dwelling place
  And be thy daily Friend!

Then go not thou in search of Him,
  But to thyself repair;
Wait thou within the silence dim,
  And thou shalt find Him there.

F. L. HOSMER

O Thou Who dwellest within, let the hush of Thy
presence fall upon me now, overcoming every stormy
part of my nature with Thy peace.

Adoration, Praise and Thanksgiving

Praise, my soul, the King of Heaven,
  To His feet thy tribute bring;
Ransomed, healed, restored, forgiven,
  Who like thee His praise should sing?
    Praise Him! Praise Him!
  Praise the everlasting King.

Praise Him for His grace and favour
  To our fathers in distress;
Praise Him, still the same for ever,
  Slow to chide and swift to bless:
    Praise Him! Praise Him!
  Glorious in His faithfulness.

Father-like He tends and spares us;
  Well our feeble frame He knows;
In His hands He gently bears us,
  Rescues us from all our foes:
    Praise Him! Praise Him!
  Widely as His mercy flows.

Angels help us to adore Him;
  Ye behold Him face to face;
Sun and moon, bow down before Him;
  Dwellers all in time and space,
    Praise Him! Praise Him!
  Praise with us the God of grace.

HENRY FRANCIS LYTE

Confession, Forgiveness and Unloading

FORGIVE US, O Lord,
For everything that has spoiled our home life:
For the moodiness and irritability which made us difficult to live with;
For the insensitiveness which made us careless of the feelings of others;
For selfishness which made life harder for others. . . .

Forgive us, O Lord,
For everything that has spoiled our witness for Thee;
That so often men would never have known that we had been with Jesus and pledged ourselves to Him:
That we have so often denied with our lives that which we said with our lips;
For the difference between our creed and our conduct, our profession and our practice;
For any example which made it easier for men to criticise Thy Church or for another to sin.

When we think of ourselves and of the meanness and ugliness and weakness of our lives, we thank Thee for Jesus Christ our Saviour. Grant unto us a true penitence for our sins. Grant that at the foot of the Cross, we may find our burdens rolled away. And so strengthen us by Thy Spirit that in the days to come, we may live more nearly as we ought. Through Jesus Christ our Lord. Amen.

WILLIAM BARCLAY

Positive Affirmation and Reception

GOD is at work at the point where my difficulties are occurring. He is Power and Health, so He is trying to overcome disease. He is Love and Serenity, so He is trying to quieten my troubled mind. He is Purpose and Plan, so He is trying to direct my will and guide me into His way.

I here and now affirm my readiness to submit to Him and to co-operate with Him, and I honestly pray to be shown where I am standing in His way and defeating Him, or where others are doing so.

I will accept only the evil which cannot be altered, and then I know He will weave that, however different from His ideal will, into His pattern of ultimate good.

Petition

THE WESTERN sky is aflame with the sunset,
Black clouds above,
Deep pools of red and orange and gold on the sky-line:
And afar, on a long, dark ridge,
Soaring aloft, stalwart and stark,
Sharp cut on that radiant sky,
A single pine-tree;

Seen from near by that tree will be black and obscure,
Undistinguished, as night comes down, from its fellows;
But thus descried, five miles away, and in front of the
    sunset
It stands sublime,
Stately and lonely and splendid,
Pointing the way to Heaven;

So also, O Master, may our lives be:
Undistinguished here from our fellows,
Obscure, unassuming and humble:
But seen from afar,
Over the long dark waste of the years,
May they stand forth clear and splendid for Thee,
Illumined, aflame, in the fire divine
Of Thy great Love,
Pointing the way unto Thee.

J. S. HOYLAND

DAY 25 ROOM 6
Intercession

I LIFT UP my heart, O God, for the mentally sick,
especially for those who today dwell in misery and
despair. Tell them in ways which may not be open to
any human friend that Thou art still with them, that
Thou wilt never leave them and that Thou canst weave
their sorrow into a plan which one day they will con-
template without regret.

In the depths of their minds, confused and unhappy
only at the surface, may spiritual progress be made and
nothing good be lost by illness. Hasten the day of recovery
and mental peace.

For those who minister to them, I also pray that they may have great patience, great pity, great forbearance, great love and great success.

May the misery of their patients never invade, so as to disable, their own minds or undermine their faith in Thy goodness. May they infect their patients with a joy that comes to them from Thee, and may they refuse to be downcast by the horror of mental illness, knowing that it is transient—however long to us it seems to last—and that the abiding things are health and joy and peace and love. Amen.

Today I lift up my heart in intercession for:

DAY 25 ROOM 7
Meditation

Now it came to pass, while the multitude pressed upon Him and heard the word of God, that He was standing by the lake of Gennesaret; and He saw two boats standing by the lake: but the fishermen had gone out of them, and were washing their nets. And He entered into one of the boats, which was Simon's, and asked him to put out a little from the land. And He sat down and taught the multitudes out of the boat. And when He had left speaking, He said unto Simon, "Put out into the deep, and let down your nets for a draught."

And Simon answered and said, "Master, we toiled all night, and took nothing: but at Thy word I will let down the nets." And when they had this done, they inclosed a great multitude of fishes; and their nets were breaking; and they beckoned unto their partners in the other boat, that they should come and help them. And they came, and filled both the boats, so that they began to sink. But Simon Peter, when he saw it, fell down at Jesus' knees, saying, "Depart from me; for I am a sinful man, O Lord." For he was amazed, and all that were with him, at the draught of the fishes which they had taken; and so were also James and John, sons of Zebedee, which were partners with Simon. And Jesus said unto Simon, "Fear not; from henceforth thou shalt catch men." And when they had brought their boats to land, they left all, and followed Him.

St. Luke 5 [1-12]

Maybe it was a miracle; a breakthrough of the supernatural. It would be presumption to determine what Jesus could and could not do. Maybe that Jesus suddenly noticed a shoal and directed the disciples so that they got their nets down into the middle of it and had to have the help of others.

I see, in imagination, the boats landing, the nets, breaking with fish, being lifted out. I note that Jesus did not mind taking life for the sake of men's physical hunger. I see impulsive Peter flinging himself down— "Depart from me, for I am a sinful man, O Lord." I know how he felt, but it was the last thing he wanted. He left his nets to follow Jesus instead and to become a fisher of men. Yet this is a Jew! If he had only followed his business instincts, he would have wanted Jesus in his business and in his boat. Here was a Man who gave directions which led to a net-breaking haul! But no, he did not seek to use Jesus to promote *his* ambitions. He deserted his ambitions to follow where Jesus led.

Dear Master, have I not often used Thee and Thy message and Thy work and Thy Church to further *my* ambitions, to exalt *my* ego. Forgive me. And from now on let me humbly follow where Thou dost lead. Let me test every activity by asking whether its motive is to exalt myself or to exalt Thee. And help me not to shun Thy lonely way even when it means suffering from which everything selfish in me shrinks away, remembering that Thy way led, not to blithe happiness among the flowers and friends of Galilee, but to the gaunt hillside outside a city, where Thine enemies mocked and scourged, thorn-crowned and crucified Thee, though Thou wert and art the Prince of Glory. Amen.

Day 26

DAY 26 ROOM I

The Affirmation of the Divine Presence

WE HAVE to remember as the main principle of the practical Christian life that we have not to work up to God through toil and discipline, till feeling comes, but we have first of all to do that which is in our power to do, to surrender the will in moral sincerity, and then to assume that God is *with us*, because He must be. This simple act of faith will not only give us a right attitude towards our feelings, but it will more quickly than anything else open the way for the feeling of the presence of God.

W. FEARON HALLIDAY

226

O somewhere, somewhere, God unknown
    Exist and be!
I am dying, I am all alone;
    I must have Thee!

God! God! My sense, my soul, my all,
    Dies in the cry:
Saw'st Thou the faint star flame and fall?
    Ah! It was I.

F. W. H. MYERS

DAY 26 ROOM 2
Adoration, Praise and Thanksgiving

WHAT SHALL I do my God to love,
    My loving God to praise?
The length, and breadth, and height to prove,
    And depth of sovereign grace?

Thy sovereign grace to all extends,
    Immense and unconfined;
From age to age it never ends;
    It reaches all mankind.

Throughout the world its breadth is known,
    Wide as infinity;
So wide it never passed by one,
    Or it had passed by me.

My trespass was grown up to heaven;
    But far above the skies,
In Christ abundantly forgiven,
    I see Thy mercies rise.

The depth of all-redeeming love
  What angel tongue can tell?
O may I to the utmost prove
  The gift unspeakable.

Come quickly, gracious Lord, and take
  Possession of Thine own;
My longing heart vouchsafe to make
  Thine everlasting throne.

CHARLES WESLEY

DAY 26 ROOM 3
Confession, Forgiveness and Unloading

NOT WHAT these hands have done
  Can save this guilty soul;
Not what this toiling flesh has borne
  Can make my spirit whole.

  Not what I feel or do
    Can give me peace with God;
Not all my prayers, and sighs, and tears
    Can bear my awful load. . . .

  Thy love to me, O God,
    Not mine, O Lord, to Thee,
Can rid me of this dark unrest,
    And set my spirit free.

Thy grace alone, O God,
    To me can pardon speak;
Thy power alone, O Son of God,
    Can this sore bondage break.

I bless the Christ of God,
    I rest on love divine,
And with unfaltering lip and heart,
    I call this Saviour mine.

HORATIUS BONAR

DAY 26 ROOM 4
Positive Affirmation and Reception

THY SEEMING denial of *my* way is Thy doorway into *Thine*. Let me walk through that doorway *with my head up*.

Wilfrid H. Bourne has pointed out the use in the letter to the Hebrews of the word "better"—"a better covenant," "a better possession," "a better country," "a better resurrection," "some better thing," etc. He adds: "Life holds the most wonderful adventures for those who can face every mysterious change in their affairs with the question, 'What better thing has God for me?' Such a self-query is not prompted by any selfish motive. We ought not to dismiss these attitudes as being the compensating qualities *designed to tone disappointment into acceptance.* . . . We can put a splendid zest into life when we turn from some apparent refusal and look for the 'better way.'"

Petition

O GOD, our Leader and our Master and our Friend, forgive our imperfections and our little motives, take us and make us one with Thy great purpose, use us and do not reject us, make us all here servants of Thy kingdom, weave our lives into Thy struggle to conquer and to bring peace and union to the world.

We are small and feeble creatures, we are feeble in speech, feebler still in action, nevertheless let but Thy light shine upon us, and there is not one of us who cannot be lit by Thy fire and who cannot lose himself in Thy salvation. Take us into Thy purposes, O God. Let Thy kingdom come into our hearts and into this world.

H. G. WELLS
The Soul of a Bishop

Intercession

FOR THE WORKERS of the world who call themselves ordinary men and women; the people who do dull, monotonous tasks which often irk them and for which there is little incentive.

That they may see all service to man as service to God. Indeed, God can be worshipped by us in solitude, but He can only be served as we serve mankind.

That they may see that all work—not inherently evil —can be service to Him, and that Christ served God just as truly in the Carpenter's shop as on the hill where He delivered the Sermon on the Mount. Indeed, *before* He had preached one sermon, the Voice said, "This is my beloved Son in Whom I am well pleased."

> Very dear the Cross of shame,
> Where He took the sinners' blame,
> And the tomb wherein He lay,
> Until the third day came;
>
> But He bore the self-same load,
> And He walked the same high road,
> When the Carpenter of Nazareth
> Made common things for God.

WALTER C. SMITH

That men may so feel that *their* job is Divine Service and offered to God, that they may offer their best, give happily an hour's service for an hour's pay and hear the Master's, "Well done!"

> If Jesus built a ship,
>   She would travel trim.
> If Jesus roofed a barn,
>   No leaks would be left by Him.
> If Jesus made a garden,
>   It would look like Paradise.
> If Jesus did my day's work,
>   It would delight His Father's eyes.

S.U.

As we pray for all the world's workers, may we in this spirit offer our day's work to Thee, O Lord!

I could not find Him where the vestured priests
    Intoned the ancient ritual of prayer.
My neighbour bowed the knee,
    And yet to me
    He was not there.

I could not find Him where the bugles called,
    And men cried "Hallelujah" to the sky.
My neighbour sobbed His name—
    To her He came
    But passed me by.

Yet on a busy day when spring winds blew
    My billowing linen to the bleaching sun,
That Man Who served with wood
    So clearly stood,
    Smiling: "Well done!"

Doris M. Holden
To Each His Vision

Today I lift up my heart in intercession for:

Meditation

H E WENT up into the mountain apart to pray, and when the even was come, He was there alone.

It is evening. The Sea of Galilee lies before your eyes. In the west the splendid scarlets and golds have faded. It is the moment of daffodil and pale-green sky. To your left, mountains run down steeply to the sea. Jesus is climbing up a spur of one of these mountains, seeking quietude in the bosom of the hills and in the hush of night; seeking to push back the tumultuous demands of all there is to do, to make a silence in which the soul can breathe, to pray. You can see His figure outlined for a moment against the fading light of that last glow of evening. But, in the east, clouds have gathered; clouds that mean storm. Rank upon rank, battalion upon battalion, they sweep westward. The water of the lake turns from amber to steel. The wind that went to summon the storm returns in front of it, majestically heralding its advent. It strikes chill and cold, menacing almost. Then the swish of the rain. Jesus hears it long before it reaches Him. He sees in front of Him a shepherd's hut on the hillside. He makes for it to avoid the discomfort of a soaking, lights the simple lamp He finds within, and kneels to pray.

Now imagine that you are on the mountain, too. The storm is on you. You see a light shining from the window of the hut. Panting and dishevelled, you rush up to it, seeking shelter. Glancing through the window, you see who is there, and you turn away. Shelter or no shelter, you feel you cannot intrude on His seclusion. But He has heard you. He rises, flings open the door. For very you

233

there is His smile, His word of welcome. Then the door closes. Just you and Jesus. Jesus and you.

I will not try to imagine what He would say to you. It would be presumptuous to do that. I don't know you. I know, I think, some of the things He would have to say to me. But you know yourself a little bit. And you know some of the things He would say to you. But if He said nothing, His presence would say everything. I think at first you would lift your eyes to His. Then somehow I think you would drop them. It is hard to look into eyes that search the uttermost depths of the heart, eyes that can see that inward rottenness, that furtive secret you have guarded from the world so long. Yet, if it be hard to look at Him, it is harder not to look at Him. After a while you would look again into those dark, clear, steady, quiet eyes, and find them not only searching, but shining; shining, not with any light regard for sin, but with a compassion that goes below the sin to the pure desire beneath. And in eyes that are the homes of all your dreams you would see the answer to all your prayers. You would *know* that He believed in you. A tremendous confidence would drive away all your fears and possess your whole being. Just because you could never belie a faith in you like His, a new faith in yourself would be born forthwith, and you would know yourself to be "able for anything." A sense of unbreakable security would possess you because you would know yourself forgiven, understood, accepted and loved.

Now the storm has passed. It is long after midnight, but you do not care. He sees you a little way on your path homewards. Then He turns back to pray. You have half a thought to go back with Him. The thought of parting seems for a moment more than you can bear. Then you feel that you never *can* really be parted from

234

Him, though He goes His way and you yours unto the end of the earth. Something marvellous has happened. He is still with you. He has not gone back after all. He is dwelling within you. There has been a new birth. He will express Himself through you. It is as though your heart has become the hut; as though you had gained Him for ever. Something mystical has happened for which there are no words. You are not just "you" any longer. You have become a self whose highest joy and truest life it will for ever be to express Jesus, and bring to others the wealth and beauty He has brought to you . . . The wind is hushed now. A crescent moon sails quietly through the last racks of storm-cloud. Here and there a star. One long, low, fading belt of light on the distant horizon. You stride back to your job again on feet that scarcely touch the mountain turf; back to a life that can never, never be the same again. For in your heart there is an inward strength, an exultant radiance, a sense of complete well-being, an outgoing love, and an ineffable peace. They do not belong to this world, and *nothing* in this world can destroy them.

"Ah," you say, "but this is imagination." The hut, the light, the mountain, yes. But not the Presence. Unless the New Testament is a lie, then this experience is for you. Perhaps it will mean a discipline, but look and listen and you will see and hear. "Our fellowship is with the Father *and with His Son Jesus Christ.*"

(from *Jesus and Ourselves*)

Dear Master, dwell in my heart all day, so that I may show forth the cheerfulness and courage which strengthen others, which lighten their load and illumine their pathway, for Thy Name's sake. Amen.

235

The Affirmation of the Divine Presence

O SON OF GOD, to right my lot,
  Naught but Thy Presence can avail:
Yet on the road Thy wheels are not,
Nor on the sea Thy sail!
My "how" or "when," Thou wilt not heed,
But come down Thine own secret stair,
That Thou may'st answer all my need,
Yea, every bygone prayer.

GEORGE MACDONALD

The angel of His presence saved them.

Isaiah 63 ⁹

O might I 'scape the sordid city air,
  This moaning human hive's unresting hum,
  Then would my soul, that pinioned is and dumb,
Shake free her wings and all her life declare.
  I will away by secret winding stair
  To my closed garden whither angels come,
Where the marred spirit, now unmanned and numb,
  May be recovered from her dark despair;
  Peace giving healing light for pitiless glare,
  Faith bringing vision to the downcast eyes,
Love heaping up the heart's spent treasuries
  Till by God's angels tended and made fair,
I mount again into life's hurrying street,
Strengthened to serve my Lord with shining feet.

W. C. BRAITHWAITE

Then the Devil leaveth Him, and behold angels came and ministered unto Him.

St. Matthew 4 ¹¹

DAY 27 ROOM 2
Adoration, Praise and Thanksgiving

O GOD, I do adore Thee and praise Thy holy name and give thanks unto Thee: For years of health, for countless occasions of happiness, for friends and fun, for the great out of doors with all its beauty and renewal, and for fireside fellowship with keen discussion, or lovely music, or silent communion of heart with heart.

I thank Thee for the intimate joy of Thy forgiveness, for every outpouring of Thy love and grace, for new beginnings, and for that joy in life that seems to break in upon me from another plane of being.

I thank Thee for all the fellowship of Thy House and for the friends I have made there, for all I have learned about Thee, for the prayers and love and sympathy of my friends, for those who have really forgiven me and overlooked my failings and not turned from me in my hour of need.

May I never, because of present sorrow, forget the gladness I have known, or lose touch with the eternal world of joy. Let memory bring the light of the past and shed it on my path in hours of darkness, that my praise and gratitude may not depend just on the present circumstances, but on what Thou eternally art. Amen.

Confession, Forgiveness and Unloading

THOU, our Elder Brother, Who
In Thy flesh our trial knew,
Thou Who hast been touched by these
Our most sad infirmities,
Thou alone the grief can span
In the dual heart of man,
And between the soul and sense
Reconcile all difference,
Change the dream of me and mine
For the truth of Thee and Thine,
And through chaos, doubt and strife
Interfuse Thy calm of life.

JOHN GREENLEAF WHITTIER

I confess to Thee, O God, the "chaos, doubt and strife" within my own heart. Thy Holy Spirit has ever sought to bring from chaos calm, from doubt assurance, and from strife peace. Let "me and mine" give place now to "Thee and Thine," and as a calm and lovely dawn follows a black night of terror and despair, so let Thy Holy Spirit dawn on my troubled heart with the assurance of forgiveness and the healing of His Peace. Amen.

Positive Affirmation and Reception

GOD IS at work *now* at the point at which I am facing difficulty or suffering or trouble. He is seeking to heal where healing is needed. He is illuminating where my way seems hidden and dark. He is strengthening where my will is weak and faltering. God is at work and God is Power and Light. He creates and sustains health and harmony.

I now affirm this and receive the truth of its message.

DAY 27 ROOM 5

Petition

TO MY GOD a heart of flame;
To my fellow men a heart of love;
To myself a heart of steel.

ST. AUGUSTINE

Lord, make me an instrument of Thy peace.
Where there is hatred, let me sow love;
Where there is injury, pardon;
Where there is doubt, faith;
Where there is despair, hope;
Where there is darkness, light;
Where there is sadness, joy.

O Divine Master, grant that
I may not so much seek
To be consoled, as to console;
Not so much to be understood as
To understand; not so much to be
Loved as to love:
For it is in giving that we receive;
It is in pardoning, that we are pardoned;
It is in dying, that we awaken to eternal life.

ST. FRANCIS OF ASSISI

Intercession

WHEN the weary, seeking rest,
 To Thy goodness flee;
When the heavy-laden cast
 All their load on Thee;
When the troubled, seeking peace,
 On Thy name shall call;
When the sinner, seeking life,
 At Thy feet shall fall:
Hear then in love, O Lord, the cry,
In heaven, Thy dwelling-place on high.

When the worldling, sick at heart,
 Lifts his soul above;
When the prodigal looks back
 To his Father's love;
When the proud man in his pride
 Stoops to seek Thy face;
When the burdened brings his guilt
 To Thy throne of grace:
Hear then in love, O Lord, the cry,
In heaven, Thy dwelling-place on high.

When the stranger asks a home,
 All his toils to end;
When the hungry craveth food,
 And the poor a friend;
When the sailor on the wave
 Bows the fervent knee;
When the soldier on the field
 Lifts his heart to Thee:
Hear then in love, O Lord, the cry,
In heaven, Thy dwelling-place on high.

When the man of toil and care,
  In the city crowd;
When the shepherd on the moor,
  Names the name of God;
When the learnèd and the high,
  Tired of earthly fame,
Upon higher joys intent,
  Name the blessed name:
Hear then in love, O Lord, the cry,
In heaven, Thy dwelling-place on high.

When the child, with grave fresh lip,
  Youth, or maiden fair,
When the agèd, weak and grey,
  Seek Thy face in prayer;
When the widow weeps to Thee,
  Sad, and lone, and low;
When the orphan brings to Thee
  All his orphan woe:
Hear then in love, O Lord, the cry,
In heaven, Thy dwelling-place on high.

When creation, in her pangs,
  Heaves her heavy groan;
When Thy Salem's exiled sons
  Breathe their bitter moan;
When Thy widowed, weeping church
  Looking for a home,
Sendeth up her silent sigh,
  Come, Lord Jesus, come!
Hear then in love, O Lord, the cry,
In heaven, Thy dwelling-place on high.

HORATIUS BONAR

Today I lift up my heart in intercession for:

Meditation

WHITHER, 'midst falling dew,
    While glow the heavens with the last steps
        of day,
Far, through their rosy depths, dost thou pursue
    Thy solitary way?

Vainly the fowler's eye
Might mark thy distant flight to do thee wrong,
As, darkly seen against the crimson sky,
    Thy figure floats along.

Seek'st thou the plashy brink
Of weedy lake, or marge of river wide,
Or where the rocking billows rise and sink
    On the chafed ocean-side?

There is a Power whose care
Teaches thy way along that pathless coast—
The desert and illimitable air—
    Lone wandering, but not lost. . . .

Thou'rt gone, the abyss of heaven
Hath swallowed up thy form; yet on my heart
Deeply has sunk the lesson thou hast given,
    And shall not soon depart.

He who, from zone to zone,
Guides through the boundless sky thy certain flight,
In the long way that I must tread alone,
    Will lead my steps aright.

WILLIAM CULLEN BRYANT
To a Waterfowl

The Affirmation of the Divine Presence

IN THE castle of my soul there is a little postern gate
Where, when I enter, I am in the presence of God.
In a moment, in a turning of a thought,
I am where God is.
When I meet God there, all life gains a new meaning,
Small things become great, and great things small,
Lowly and despised things are shot through with glory.

My troubles seem but the pebbles on the road,
My joys seem like the everlasting hills,
All my fever is gone in the great peace of God,
And I pass through the door from Time into Eternity.

WALTER RAUSCHENBUSCH

I am not alone
By night,
Or by day,
Or by circumstance;
Neither in the silence,
Nor in the city's roar;
Nor as I lie
At the door of death,
Or stand on the
Threshold
Of a new life;
For Thou art *with me*
Around me,
Underneath me,
Bearing me up,
Giving me strength,
Luring me on.

I am not alone;
Thou hast been,
Thou wilt be,
Thou art
With me.
Lo, I am always in Thy care. Amen.

SAMUEL F. PUGH

DAY 28 ROOM 2
Adoration, Praise and Thanksgiving

THE SPACIOUS firmament on high,
With all the blue ethereal sky,
And spangled heavens, a shining frame,
Their great Original proclaim.
The unwearied sun, from day to day,
Doth his Creator's power display;
And publishes to every land
The work of an almighty hand.

Soon as the evening shades prevail,
The moon takes up the wondrous tale,
And nightly to the listening earth
Repeats the story of her birth:
While all the stars that round her burn,
And all the planets in their turn,
Confirm the tidings as they roll,
And spread the truth from pole to pole.

What though in solemn silence all
Move round this dark terrestrial ball;
What though no real voice nor sound
Amidst their radiant orbs be found:
In reason's ear they all rejoice,
And utter forth a glorious voice,
For ever singing as they shine:
The hand that made us is divine!

JOSEPH ADDISON

DAY 28 ROOM 3
Confession, Forgiveness and Unloading

THOU KNOWEST, Lord, the weariness and sorrow
    Of the sad heart that comes to Thee for rest;
Cares of today, and burdens for tomorrow,
    Blessings implored, and sins to be confessed;
We come before Thee at Thy gracious word,
And lay them at Thy feet: Thou knowest, Lord.

Thou knowest all the past: how long and blindly
    On the dark mountains the lost wanderer strayed;
How the good Shepherd followed, and how kindly
    He bore it home, upon His shoulders laid,
And healed the bleeding wounds, and soothed the pain,
And brought back life, and hope, and strength again.

Thou knowest all the present: each temptation,
    Each toilsome duty, each foreboding fear;
All to each one assigned of tribulation,
    Or to beloved ones than self more dear;
All pensive memories, as we journey on,
Longings for vanished smiles and voices gone.

Thou knowest all the future: gleams of gladness
    By stormy clouds too quickly overcast;
Hours of sweet fellowship, and parting sadness,
    And the dark river to be crossed at last.
O what could hope and confidence afford
To tread that path but this—Thou knowest, Lord?

Thou knowest, not alone as God, all knowing;
    As Man our mortal weakness Thou hast proved;
On earth, with purest sympathies o'erflowing,
    O Saviour, Thou hast wept, and Thou hast loved;
And love and sorrow still to Thee may come,
And find a hiding-place, a rest, a home.

Therefore we come, Thy gentle call obeying,
    And lay our sins and sorrows at Thy feet,
On everlasting strength our weakness staying,
    Clothed in Thy robe of righteousness complete;
Then rising and refreshed we leave Thy throne,
And follow on to know as we are known.

JANE L. BORTHWICK

DAY 28 ROOM 4
Positive Affirmation and Reception

ALL EMOTIONS hostile to Thy will, and therefore to
my welfare, are being dissolved and washed out of
my deep mind by the inflowing of Thy cleansing and
renewing love.

Petition

GRANT, O Lord, that when I feel irritated by trifling annoyances, by temporary frustrations, by little things to which I must give time and attention when big things are on my mind and clamour for quiet thought and planning, I may maintain a quiet heart and a cheerful readiness to do what the moment demands.

Let me recall the Carpenter at Nazareth Who must often have longed for the quiet of the Galilean hills and been frustrated by the last-minute customer, demanding that this plough be mended or that yoke planed smooth.

Let me realise that it was in situations like these that He became disciplined to patience and learned how to maintain His inward peace. Was it then that He gained *authority* to say, "Come unto Me! I will refresh you" to those who are fretful and heavy laden? Was it because He accepted the belated customer's yoke as His Father's will at that moment that He could say, "Take My yoke —as I used to take the yokes of others as My Father's will —and you will find that it doesn't chafe you. I know how to 'ease' and adjust the yoke that never can be 'easy,' so that it does not rub and chafe the shoulders, and I bear the heavy end of every yoke Myself. Take up the burden as if it were Mine and you will find it light, and I will share it with you. Be meek and lowly-hearted, and in the midst of fretfulness you will find your mind at rest"?

O Christ, Who didst learn so much at a carpenter's bench, let me hear Thee saying once more, "Come unto Me, all ye that labour and are heavy laden, and I will give you rest. Take My yoke upon you and learn of Me;

for I am meek and lowly of heart: and ye shall find rest unto your souls. For My yoke is easy and My burden is light."[1]

DAY 28 ROOM 6
Intercession

O GOD, our Father, we lift up in intercession the cause of Christ throughout the world. We thank Thee for every messenger who has carried the good news to the end of the earth, and we thank Thee that Thy messengers have such good news to carry.

Where Thy servants in far-off places are lonely, or dispirited, may the vision of Christ, the memory of His call and the remembrance of our love and our support in prayer fill their hearts with new courage. Unite Thy Church throughout the world in one grand aim to bring Christ to the hearts of men, and use every one of us, we pray Thee, in that mighty purpose for which Thy dear Son was willing to die. We ask it through Jesus Christ our Lord. Amen.

Today I lift up my heart in intercession for:

---

[1] See *Matthew* 11 28–30. The Greek word for "easy" means "well-adjusted." I have read that carpenters' shops in ancient Palestine frequently bore notices carrying the slogan, "My yokes are well-adjusted." Jesus may have been quoting from a notice outside His father's shop.

Meditation

THERE was a time when pain and sorrow seemed to me intolerable intruders. I still want to cast them out. Yet they, too, while not His agents, are made His instruments. Life seems nobler and braver because of them. Does God use something whose actuality He did not plan, to deepen the lives He loves? In present conditions can we have the finest things flowering in personality if the Cross is removed from life? We must fight pain and sorrow, yes, but what cannot be overcome in that sense can be overcome in another. The liability can be turned to asset, the heavy, dull lead into shining gold.

Some time ago I stayed in a congenial home, one of those homes that *receive* you at once. My hostess was an artist. When I sat down to the first meal I did not know this fact. But hanging on the wall opposite where I sat at table was a beautiful picture. It was an interior full of firelight and glow and rich colour—full of peace. I could not help saying, "What a beautiful picture!" Then I learnt that it was the work of my hostess.

Next to it on the wall was a picture with a very different subject; the sea. In the left-hand corner was just the nose of a boat. To the right was a rather rickety landing-stage. It had a lamp on a high pole at the seaward end. Most of the canvas was of sea and sky, but with little colour. It was no painting of sunset or sunrise. The first impression was of gloomy mist, grey water, a bleak discomfort. It made one feel forlorn and depressed. When I asked who painted it, I was told a name which we will call Watson. I knew the name and knew the man and knew that he had had pictures in the Royal

Academy. I did not know then that he had taught my hostess to paint.

"Why does a man take a depressing subject like that for a picture?" I asked stupidly, as we rose from a meal.

"Yes," said another guest at the table, "Watson has progressed since he painted that."

We adjourned to the drawing-room. No more was said then. But at a subsequent meal I sat and looked at the picture. It had grown on me during the night! It was beginning to talk to me. I went away and came back to it yet again. At last I said to my host, "That picture appeals to me more the more I look at it." I can see his slow, delightful smile now. "Yes," he said quietly, "it is a good picture." I felt he was letting me down lightly for having made such a stupid and superficial remark about it earlier!

I still think his wife's picture wonderfully good, but wife and husband and guest would agree that Watson's picture is greater. The boat, the lamp, the landing-stage: man's pathetic symbols of safety; the expressions of man's instinct for comfort, for the familiar, for security, for what I want to call compassability, in conparison with the infinite ocean in the background, so vast; symbol of the eternity so close to us, with all that the sea suggests of distressing immensities before which, man has, in a sense, to bow the head and acknowledge unfathomable mystery and overwhelming power. The picture thrust upon one what one cannot really shut out, the misty loneliness, the desolation, the void of infinitude, the immemorial pain of man.

We like the warm interior of a cosy room. We like to fasten the windows and draw the curtains on a night of storm, to crouch before the fire, to build it up with logs so that the crackling flames and the bright room may dull our senses to the beating of the rain on the panes and the moaning of the wind about the house. Yet, somehow, we have to make terms with the storm. We cannot blot it out or live as though it were not. Somehow we must take it into our hearts. No harmony, no depth of character is possible to one who runs away from life, shuts his ears to its anguish and his heart to its pain. And, battling with the storm, we shall get exhausted and probably wounded. Yet it is better so. Can one think of great music without anguish, great poetry without sorrow, great art without agony, great living which has never opened the door to pain?

It was in the Garden of Gethsemane late one night that I learnt that lesson, saw, dimly and imperfectly, that glimpse of a vision. My friends and I had travelled from Jerusalem on one wonderful moonlight night, planning to be under the olive trees at about the same time as the Master prayed there on the night before His death. We separated in the garden and each knelt down under the silver shimmer of "the little grey leaves." It must have been midnight when we started back. I went home to bed at last in a charming room in a cathedral garden at Jerusalem. But I shall never forget the night that I spent amongst the trees near the garden of sorrow. Gethsemane yielded to me a tiny fraction of her agelong secret—the secret which the olives whisper to one another in the wind that stirs before the dawn, when "the little grey leaves," dying, fall back gently upon the breast of the earth, their mother who gave them birth, and who, in some form of resurrection, will use their present dying, which now seems so unutterably and relentlessly sad, to enrich the earth.

from *It Happened in Palestine*

Into the woods my Master went,
  Clean forspent, forspent.
Into the woods my Master came,
  Forspent with love and shame;
But the olives were not blind to Him,
The little grey leaves were kind to Him,
The thorn tree had a mind to Him,
  When into the woods He came.

Out of the woods my Master went,
  And He was well content,
Out of the woods my Master came,
  Content with death and shame;
And when death and shame would woo Him, last,
From under the trees they drew Him, last,
And on a tree they slew Him, last,
  When out of the woods He came.

SIDNEY LANIER

A Ballad of Trees and the Master

"He was well content." Grant to me, also, O dear Master, in my trifling Gethsemanes, the secret of that deep and final contentment and the holy sacrament of Thy peace.

Day 29

The Affirmation of the Divine Presence

IF WE desire to enter into our supernatural inheritance, the deep tranquility of faith, coming unto God, we must be completely absorbed by the thought that He is; and rewards, in such ways as we can endure, them—and them only—that diligently seek Him for His own sake alone.

EVELYN UNDERHILL

Adoration, Praise and Thanksgiving

GOD, the God I love and worship, reigns in sorrow
on the Tree,
Broken, bleeding, but unconquered; Very God of God
to me,
In a manger, in a cottage, in an honest workman's shed,
In the homes of humble peasants and the simple lives
they lead;
In the life of One, an outcast and a vagabond on earth,
In the common things He valued and proclaimed of
countless worth;
And above all, in the horror of the cruel death He died,
Thou hast bid us seek Thy glory in the criminal crucified;
And we find it—for Thy glory is the glory of love's loss,
And Thou hast no other splendour than the splendour
of the Cross.

G. A. STUDDERT KENNEDY

I adore and praise and thank thee, O God, that in
Christ crucified, Thou didst reveal the fact that the very
essence of Thy nature is a Love that will go to the
uttermost for every man.

Confession, Forgiveness and Unloading

THE LORD will save His people here;
In times of need their help is near
To all by sin and hell oppressed;
And they that know Thy name will trust
In Thee, who, to Thy promise just,
Hast never left a soul distressed.

The Lord is by His judgments known;
He helps His poor afflicted one,
  His sorrows all He bears in mind;
The mourner shall not always weep,
Who sows in tears in joy shall reap,
  With grief who seeks, with joy shall find.

A helpless soul that looks to Thee
Is sure at last Thy face to see,
  And all Thy goodness to partake;
The sinner who for Thee doth grieve,
And longs, and labours to believe,
  Thou never, never wilt forsake.

CHARLES WESLEY

DAY 29 ROOM 4
Positive Affirmation and Reception

WE LIKE to think of what has been given as having been acquired. We take our nature for our own work, and our lot in life for our own conquest—an illusion born of vanity. . . . We are unwilling to be the product of our circumstances, or the mere expression of an inner germ. And yet we have received everything, and the part which is really ours is small indeed, for it is mostly made up of negation, resistance, faults. We receive everything, both life and happiness; but the manner in which we receive, this is what is still ours. Let us then receive trustfully without shame or anxiety. Let us humbly accept from God even our own nature, and treat it charitably, firmly, intelligently. Not that we are called upon to accept the evil and the disease in us, but let us accept ourselves in spite of the evil and the disease. . . . Above all [ask] for the spirit of joy and gratitude—

that genuine and religious optimism which sees in God a Father. We must dare to be happy, and dare to confess it, regarding ourselves always as the depositories, not as the authors of our own joy.

AMIEL, *Journal*, 14th May, 1852

So much, O God, I have received, let me receive as from Thy hand, the gift of this new day and affirm now Thy power to make of it something worthy to be offered to Thee at eventide.

DAY 29 ROOM 5
Petition

LORD GOD, Thou knowest that my deepest need is not to learn more about Thee, not to understand more, not to fill my brain with more and more religious ideas, but to have the courage to put a very few ideas into practice in my way of living; not to say more and more prayers, but to become the answer to them; not to attend more and more services, but to act in a Christlike way in every circumstance in which I find myself.

O God, help me with the deed, and the word, and the daily life! Let me accept Thy way not only in intellect and feeling, but in terms of the will. There lies my bitter need. Help me for Thy name's sake. Amen.

DAY 29 ROOM 6
Intercession

LORD JESUS, I pray for those who suffer shame for Thy name. I pray for those who belong to despised and persecuted Churches. I think especially of those in

255

India, Africa and China who try to maintain their discipleship with the whole trend and weight of the opinion of the majority against them. Make them conscious of the enfolding and sustaining fellowship of the world-family of the lovers of Thy name.

I pray for those who in their own homes meet with indifference and sometimes scorn, and those who have let it be known at their work that they are on Thy side, and then found themselves unpopular, despised, and always placed in the bright light of others' watchfulness, made to beat upon them by those who wickedly *hope* for their failure that they may hold them up to derision, and escape Thy challenge themselves. For all who bravely maintain a lonely witness unsupported by Christian companionship, I lift up my heart to Thee Who didst bear the derisive mockery of Scribes and Pharisees who set out to trap Thee.

Where missionaries are exposed to the clever arguments of the hostile; where men and women love Thee sincerely, but cannot argue effectively for Thy cause; where the ageing saint or young disciple is excluded from fellowship and regarded as fogey, or crank, or spoilsport for Thy sake, O Lord Christ, show them Thy understanding love and draw very near to them in compensating compassion. Let them in no wise lose their reward. For Thy name's sake. Amen.

Today I lift up my heart in intercession for:

Meditation

CONTESSINA, forgive an old man's babble. But I am your friend, and my love for you goes deep. There is nothing I can give you which you have not got; but there is much, very much, that, while I cannot give it, you can take. No heaven can come to us unless our hearts find rest in it today. Take heaven. No peace lies in the future which is not hidden in this present little instant. Take peace!

The gloom of the world is but a shadow. Behind it, yet within our reach is joy. There is radiance and glory in the darkness, could we but see; and to see we have only to look. Contessina, I beseech you to look.

Life is so generous a giver, but we, judging its gifts by their covering, cast them away as ugly or heavy or hard. Remove the covering, and you will find beneath it a living splendour, woven of love, by wisdom, with power. Welcome it, grasp it, and you touch the angel's hand that brings it to you. Everything we call a trial, a sorrow, or a duty, believe me, that angel's hand is there; the gift is there, and the wonder of an overshadowing presence. Our joys, too; be not content with them as joys. They, too, conceal diviner gifts.

Life is so full of meaning and purpose, so full of beauty (beneath its covering) that you will find earth but cloaks your heaven. Courage, then, to claim it; that is all! But courage you have; and the knowledge that we are pilgrims together, wending through unknown country, home.

S. U.

(letter written by a priest in 1513)

257

The Affirmation of the Divine Presence

THERE is no place
Where God is not;
Wherever I go, there God is.
Now and always He upholds
Me with His power,
And keeps me safe in
His Love.

S.U.

There can be all the difference in the world between beginning a prayer with "O Almighty God" and beginning it with "Thou," breathed to Someone—*there*. We need to practise that, until the Presence becomes so real that He is in deed and truth possessing the very centre where for us the important "I" stands so supreme.

FLORENCE ALLSHORN
The Notebooks of Florence Allshorn

DAY 30 ROOM 2

Adoration, Praise and Thanksgiving

WHAT SHALL I do my God to love,
My Saviour, and the world's, to praise?
Whose tenderest compassions move
To me and all the fallen race,
Whose mercy is divinely free
For all the fallen race and—me.

I long to know, and to make known,
  The heights and depths of love divine,
The kindness Thou to me hast shown,
  Whose every sin was counted Thine:
My God for me resigned His breath;
He died to save my soul from death.

How shall I thank Thee for the grace
  On me and all mankind bestowed?
O that my every breath were praise!
  O that my heart were filled with God!
My heart would then with love o'erflow,
And all my life Thy glory show.

CHARLES WESLEY

DAY 30 ROOM 3
Confession, Forgiveness and Unloading

WE HAD no need of faith in those young days
    When we went forth on the world's unknown
  ways,
When joy from every fount of life welled out,
And beauty over-ran its crystal springs.
We could not ask if life were good or ill
When all our dreams it promised to fulfil.
We could not fear the unknown road, nor doubt
That love divine was at the heart of things.

S. R. LYSAGHT
The Test of Faith

But now, O Lord, we need faith more than we need anything. What we thought was faith was health and youth and high spirits and success and confidence, based on an abysmal ignorance of the terrible things that can happen.

We confess our utter need.
Forgive us and help us.

"When I'm alone"—the words tripped off his tongue
As though to be alone were nothing strange.
"When I was young," he said, "when I was young" . . .
I thought of age, and loneliness and change.
I thought how strange we grow when we're alone,
And how unlike the selves that meet and talk,
And blow the candle out, and say goodnight.
Alone. . . . The word is life endured and known.
It is the stillness where our spirits walk
And all but inmost faith is overthrown.

SIEGFRIED SASSOON

DAY 30 ROOM 4
Positive Affirmation and Reception

THE ECHOES of Despair slunk away, for the laugh of a brave, strong heart is death to them.

OLIVE SCHREINER

Today, I laugh!

I lift my heart to Thee,
  Saviour divine;
For Thou art all to me,
  And I am Thine.
Is there on earth a closer bond than this:
That my Beloved's mine, and I am His?

Thine am I by all ties;
  But chiefly Thine,
That through Thy sacrifice
  Thou, Lord, art mine.
By Thine own cords of love, so sweetly wound
Around me, I to Thee am closely bound. . . .

How can I, Lord, withhold
  Life's brightest hour
From Thee; or gathered gold,
  Or any power?
Why should I keep one precious thing from Thee,
When Thou hast given Thine own dear self for me?

CHARLES E. MUDIE

DAY 30 ROOM 5
Petition

FOR MORNING

ALMIGHTY God, Who hast safely brought us to the beginning of this day, defend us in the same by Thy mighty power, and grant that this day we fall into no sin, neither run into any kind of danger, but that all our doings may be ordered by Thy governance to do always that is righteous in Thy sight. Through Jesus Christ our Lord. Amen.

The Book of Common Prayer

FOR EVENING

Father in heaven, Who hast brought us unto the closing of the day, let the peace of eventide descend upon us. May every stormy passion be subdued, every unquiet thought cast out, every earthly care and anxiety forgotten, that in the calm of Thy loving presence we may find a remedy for our soul's unrest, and in Thy loving-kindness an answer to our every need. Hear us, we humbly beseech Thee, for Jesus' sake. Amen.

S.U.

DAY 30 ROOM 6
Intercession

WE LIFT up our hearts in intercession for those who find their greatest difficulties in their own homes. We pray:

For those who minister to ageing relatives who seem difficult to live with. Give them patience and sympathy, O God.

For those who are trying to bring up young children and are over-anxious about them. Give them a more carefree trust in Thee.

For those in whose homes young people are growing up, self-assertive and hostile to all restraint or advice. Give them a right understanding of liberty and a new belief in youth.

For those who are married but have ceased truly to

love, who maintain a conventional sham, but conceal a bored distaste. Give them a willingness to see the best in one who has become unattractive, a readiness to end the pride that will not talk things out and confess failure, a new realisation that their partner is disappointed too and had hoped that love would become companionship and make beautiful a serene old age.

For those who are aged and who feel unwanted, unloved and in the way. Give them to try, by humour and patience, by resolutely refusing to grumble and complain, by seeking ever to minister where they can to those with whom they live, to become lovable assets of the life of the home, beloved and admired as those are who seek to love, more than to be loved, and to serve, rather than to be served, to laugh rather than to moan.

To all these reveal Thyself as One Who understands and cares and loves; One Who can guide and sustain, and share every burden; One Who can help us back to humour and to inward peace. Remove fear and bitterness and self-pity from all our hearts and grant us Thy peace. Amen.

Today I lift up my heart in intercession for:

Meditation

ENGRAVED on a stone in a vast desert are the words:

"This too will pass."

When the light fails on winter evenings
And the river makes no sound in its passing
Behind the house, is silent but for its cold
Flowing, its reeds frozen stiffer than glass,
How can one anticipate the dawn, a sudden
Blazing of sunlight thawing the harshest sky?
How can one remember summer evenings?
Must not the tired heart sink and must not fear
Bite, like an acid, wrinkles in its stone?

Behind drawn curtains, gazing at the fire,
Think how the earth springs dumb and bound
By iron chains of frost through death-still air;
And how in every street the sealed windows
Are orange cubes of firelight, how in houses
Cuckoo-clocks imitate the Spring, candles are
Suns. Perpetual winter never known
Families warm their hands and wait, nor
Ever doubt the seasons' transience.

DAVID GASCOYNE
Perpetual Winter Never Known

While the earth remaineth, seedtime and harvest and
cold and heat, and summer and winter, and day and
night shall not cease. *Genesis* 8 [22]

O Wind,
If Winter comes, can Spring be far behind?

SHELLEY
Ode to the West Wind

The Affirmation of the Divine Presence

Enter this door
As if the floor
Within were gold,
And every wall
Of jewels all
Of wealth untold;
As if a choir
In robes of fire
Were singing here.
Nor shout, nor rush,
But hush . . .
For God is here.

JAMES MACKAY

DAY 31 ROOM 2

Adoration, Praise and Thanksgiving

This, this is the God we adore,
 Our faithful, unchangeable Friend;
Whose love is as great as His power,
 And neither knows measure nor end.

'Tis Jesus, the first and the last,
   Whose Spirit shall guide us safe home;
We'll praise Him for all that is past,
   And trust Him for all that's to come."

JOSEPH HART

We are of them that feel and cannot sing,
But sometimes, when a summer day is done,
And, wandering over field and hill, we see
White clover in a wilderness of grass,
Our hearts are bursting so with joy and love
That words must come—and in the evening calm
We cannot but stammer out, with faltering lips,
A quiet hymn of thankfulness to God.

VICTOR GOLLANCZ
My Dear Timothy

DAY 31 ROOM 3
Confession, Forgiveness and Unloading

DEAR LORD, forgive me in that so much of my religion is concerned with myself. *I* want harmony with Thee. *I* want peace of mind. *I* want health of body—and so I pray.

Too little have I cared about my brother's needs. My own burdens have seemed so obsessive that I have thought too little of theirs. Sometimes I have served others so as to gain their goodwill and their love for which I crave.

Forgive me, for I have made Thee the means and myself the end.

I know it will take long to wean me from this terrible

self-concern, but O God, help me, for Hell can be nothing else but a life of which self is the centre.

Can I ever abandon self as men a sinking ship, only to find that the waves will bear them up and a divine hand will rescue them? My salvation can come only from Thee, O Lord. Leave me not. Forgive and uphold me and make me truly Thine in utter committal to Thee. Amen.

DAY 31 ROOM 4
Positive Affirmation and Reception

I HERE quietly affirm that God is a God of Beauty. He made either alone or in co-operation with man, all beautiful forms, all groupings of colour, all that is lovely in sound.

He gave me my senses, and because eye and ear bring me the recognition and thrill of beauty, they bring me into a sense of kinship with Him. Animals may see the flowers and the sunset, but they experience—as far as we know—no reactive thrill of joy at the sight. So beauty is like the voice of a friend whispering my name, calling me to recognise kinship, reminding me that I *belong* to God.

In some moods the world seems as ugly and hostile as a vast labour-camp where we endlessly toil with meagre result and little joy, but beauty, or rather my recognition of it, is as though amid all the hostility and ugliness, I recognised the glance of a friend or felt the secret pressure of a friendly hand, and knew that I was not really alone or forlorn.

So I may affirm that the Mind and Hand that spilled, so unnecessarily and without any utilitarian reason, such loveliness as we see in Nature, cannot think less of men

267

than of lilies, cannot but desire man's response in terms of a life made beautiful by holiness instead of ugly with sin. The Heart that planned a rose cannot be unfriendly or callous, let alone hostile. "Such careful fashioning of beauty could not come from One Who at the same time could create *a man* and leave his life and destiny to the mercy of chance and destructive forces."[1]

"If I give you a rose," said Tertullian, "you cannot doubt God any more." So I will ponder again on the beauty of Nature. It points to One Who will always care more for men than for lilies and birds. ("Are ye not much better than they?")

O God, when life is hard, circumstances hostile and the heavens seem as indifferent as brass, let this affirmation deepen my trust in Thee!

DAY 31 ROOM 5
Petition

I PRAY, O Lord, that today I may know with keener awareness that I am in Thy hands; well or ill, happy or sad, at work or at play, with others or alone, may I become increasingly conscious that I dwell within Thy purposeful providence.

Illness does not mean punishment or Thy disfavour. Fun is not "secular." The trifles of my life do not forfeit Thine interest in me.

Grant me the sense of Thy presence, born of Thine indwelling and of Thine enfolding love, and let me increasingly pause to recollect that, in every circumstance, I live within Thy life and am always the object of Thy care.

[1] Professor H. H. Farmer, in *Things Not Seen* (Nisbet), to which book I am indebted here.

The perilous barque of my life has been launched on the sea of Thy life, and no ship, go where it may, can sail off the ocean.

"I cannot drift
Beyond His love and care."

If this day brings storm or stress, fear or sorrow, pain or disappointment, or if this day brings gladness, serenity, happiness and peace, let nothing rob me of the joy of knowing that I *belong* to Thee. Amen.

DAY 31 ROOM 6
Intercession

FOR CIVIC LEADERS

WE LIFT up our hearts, O Lord, in intercession for all who carry civic and political responsibilities. For all whose words and acts and lives mould public life, we offer prayer.

May they, putting aside all merely selfish ambition, seek to be the instruments of Thy will and carry out Thy purpose for the welfare of Thy people.

May Thy grace sustain them, Thy love work through them, Thy power uphold them, and may they both seek and see Thy glory in happier human lives. Through Jesus Christ our Lord. Amen.

Today I lift up my heart in intercession for:

Meditation

IT IS A form of sin to conjure up in the mind imaginative pictures in which we do that which, in our best moments, we hate ourselves for doing, for we are to love God with all our minds.

So much it is easy to concede. We sometimes, however, forget that it is a form of sin—the sin of pride—to keep alive in the memory by repeated stimulation, the imaginative pictures of regretted and forgiven sins, using those memories as whips with which to lash ourselves. We say to ourselves, "I will punish myself with remorseful memories and bring back those feelings of hot shame, for I deserve to be punished."

The angels must look on in amazement, nudge one another and say, "Why does he do that to himself? God has forgiven him all. Why doesn't he throw his whips away and go on?"

We should remember that by our self-punishment we do not render ourselves *worthy* of forgiveness. We can never "atone" for sin, or expiate it by good works, or balance the account by subsequent goodness, or get right with God while wilfully "wrong" with another person. Forgiveness cannot be merited, or earned, or won. Pride says it can, but pride *lies*. Forgiveness can only be accepted in humility and loving—not cringing—gratitude. It is a gift of God, and a gift is not earned; it is accepted and taken.

True, we live in a world of cause and effect, and forgiveness does not obliterate all the effects of our sin, though, be it remembered, it obliterates the most important and sinister effects of sin, namely, separation from God, and progressive deterioration of character, and because we find forgiveness, we may well lose those consequences which guilt and fear make permanent. The physical, mental and spiritual parts of man are so inextricably related that none can say to what extent any area of our life may be affected for good by the release of grace which forgiveness achieves. Men have found the healing of physical disease by realising the forgiveness of their sins. Christ often says, "Thy sins are forgiven thee, rise up and walk."

Those effects or consequences of sin which remain, we must accept, but not resentfully, as if they were the vengeance of an outraged, unloving Deity or the consequence of a blind nemesis.

We are to accept the consequences of forgiven sin rather as an athlete accepts the limitations imposed on him. He may not do what others do—for example, in the food he eats and the hours he keeps—but he keeps a discipline with acceptance—not rebellion—that he may achieve victory in a contest.

Being an athlete has to be paid for. Being a forgiven sinner has to be paid for. But both are payments willingly made because they buy what, in its best moments, the disciplined self desires.

Our past sins, though forgiven, impose a discipline called—if you like—the effects of sin in a law-governed universe. But that discipline can make us win what God wants us yet to achieve and to become. If we see that, we can use that imposed discipline for Him, and for our own highest good we shall accept it and cease to rebel against it.

The Prodigal did not in one moment throw off the evil effects of his sojourn in the far country. There was a convalescence, and a period of re-adjustment for body, mind and spirit. But *in one moment* he was truly at home with his Father, not abroad amongst swine. The moment his Father's arms went round him, he knew that the old relationship was restored. So may we.

And the very heart of forgiveness is not to be let off the consequences of sin, but to be restored into a relationship as intimate and loving as though sin had never broken it, so that the soul can look at God and say, "There is nothing between us." Indeed, sin, when it is forgiven, often wakens men to all that they have missed, and they enter an even richer fellowship with God than before. This is another way in which "He maketh the wrath of man to praise Him."

> In wonder lost, with trembling joy
> We take the pardon of our God.

For a Sunday

FOR A SUNDAY ROOM I
The Affirmation of the Divine Presence

I, JOHN, your brother and partaker with you in the tribulation and kingdom and patience of Jesus Christ . . . was in the Spirit on the Lord's day and I heard behind me a great voice, as of a trumpet saying, "I am the Alpha and Omega, the first and the last, the beginning and the ending, saith the Lord, which is, and which was, and which is to come, the Almighty. . . ." And He laid His right hand upon me, saying unto me, "Fear not; I am the first and the last. I am He that liveth and was dead; and behold I am alive for evermore."

Revelation 1 [9, 10, 17, 18]

The Son of Man is Lord even of the Sabbath.

St. Mark 2 [28]

Adoration, Praise and Thanksgiving

JESUS WE love to meet
  On this Thy holy day;
We worship round Thy seat
  On this Thy holy day.
Thou tender, heavenly Friend,
To Thee our prayers ascend;
Over our spirits bend
  On this Thy holy day.

We dare not trifle now
  On this Thy holy day;
In silent awe we bow
  On this Thy holy day.
Check every wandering thought,
And let us all be taught
To serve Thee as we ought
  On this Thy holy day.

We listen to Thy Word
  On this Thy holy day;
Bless all that we have heard
  On this Thy holy day;
Go with us when we part,
And to each longing heart
Thy saving grace impart
  On this Thy holy day.

ELIZABETH PARSON
(adapted in vv. 1 and 3)

Confession, Forgiveness and Unloading

O SAVIOUR Christ, Who, as Thy custom was, didst go to the synagogue on the Sabbath day to worship God and to join in the praises and prayers of His people, be with me as I go, alas in such a different spirit. Thou didst go in gay and royal gladness, unmarred by sin. I go bowed down by memories of sin and slackness, of shame and defeat hanging over me from the week that is past. Forgive me. Comfort me. Restore and renew me. I, too, would praise God with a glad heart and free.

Yet, was not even Thy gladness saddened by the state of those around Thee? Kneeling among them, did not Thy tender heart ache for their sorrows and mourn for their sins? Did not the evil of the world invade Thy soul, O Thou Who didst cry that bitter cry, "O Jerusalem, Jerusalem, how often would I have gathered thy children together, even as a hen gathereth her chickens under her wings, but ye would not . . ."?

Make this day for me a day of Forgiveness and of Peace, a day of Light and Joy. Meet with me, and with all who worship with me, in the hush of the Holy Place, and send us out, our sins forgiven, our burdens lifted, our hearts comforted, ready to step out into the world tomorrow with lighter hearts and firmer faith; with resolute wills and indomitable courage, so that, though evil seems so strong, and we are often dismayed by its strength and extent, we may not fail Thee in the part which Thou hast allotted to us in the redemption of Thy world. Amen.

O my Father, let me unload my heart today of its burdens; the burden of my own sin, the dismay at the world's widespread evil, the doubts that invade my heart, the cares of my work, the apprehension regarding the future. Let me gaze upon Thee until the sense of Thy love and majesty, Thy competence and power, soak into my soul and enable me truly to worship Thee in spirit and in truth. Amen.

FOR A SUNDAY ROOM 4
Positive Affirmation and Reception

THIS IS the day that the Lord hath made. I will rejoice and be glad in it. I now affirm and receive the gladness which this day was meant to bring.

> Let me with my heart today,
> Holy, holy, holy, singing,
>   Rapt awhile from earth away,
> All my soul to Thee upspringing,
>   Have a foretaste inly given
>   How they worship Thee in heaven. . . .
>
> Hence all care and vanity,
> For the day to God is holy; —
>   Come, Thou glorious Majesty,
> Deign to fill this temple lowly;
>   Nought today my soul shall move
>   Simply resting in Thy love.

BENJAMIN SCHMOLCK
(tr. by Catherine Winkworth)

FOR A SUNDAY ROOM 5
Petition

HELP ME, O Lord, as Sabbaths come and go, to meditate on that unseen world of the spirit, from which I have come and to which I go.

Help me to use the hours of worship and the opportunity for meditation, so that I lay hold afresh on the eternal values and increase my awareness of spiritual reality.

Help me to worship Thee today in such a spirit of gladness and sincerity, and to receive at Thy hands such spiritual enrichment, that increasingly I shall look forward to the privileges and joys of this Thy day as tired eyes look for the morning and as the weary traveller longs for home.

So, at last, when the friendly Angel of Death summons me, I shall rise up gladly, without fear, knowing that the tiresome weekdays of life are over and there begins an unending Sabbath of worship, fellowship and service in Thy dear name.

> He lifts me to the golden doors;
> The flashes come and go;
> All heaven bursts her starry floors,
> And strows her light below,
> And deepens on and up! the gates
> Roll back and far within
> For me the Heavenly Bridegroom waits,
> To make me pure of sin.
> The Sabbaths of Eternity,
> One Sabbath deep and wide—
> A light upon the shining sea—
> The Bridegroom with His bride!

ALFRED, LORD TENNYSON
St. Agnes' Eve

Then shall I see, and hear, and know
All I desired and wished below;
And every power find sweet employ
In that eternal world of joy.

ISAAC WATTS

FOR A SUNDAY ROOM 6
Intercession

FOR ALL who, in any denomination and in any form of faith, seek God today, that asking, they may receive, and seeking, they may find, and knocking, they may enter in.

For all who conduct worship today, that their entire personalities may so radiate God's presence and love, that even if their words be poor—as all words are—none shall miss a blessing or fail to find pardon, love, welcome, strength, and that portion of the unsearchable riches of Christ which represents the desire of God for him.

Today I lift up my heart in intercession for:

FOR A SUNDAY ROOM 7
Meditation

HE CAME to Nazareth, where He had been brought up: and He entered as His custom was into the synagogue on the Sabbath day . . . and the eyes of all in the synagogue were fastened on Him.

St. Luke 4 [16 and 20]

In imagination I am in the synagogue, too, waiting for the service to begin. I am spiritually hungry, longing for some message from God, some assurance that man is not left alone. Then Jesus enters. I see His quiet, yet radiant, face. I note the serenity of His whole bearing. He kneels and then sits, relaxed and happy to be with God's people on God's day. I find myself wishing He were nearer to me. Yet His entry has made a difference to us all. The whole spiritual temperature has risen. A strange sense of quiet joy and well-being seems to seep into my heart. I become sure of God and sure that I am forgiven, loved, understood, accepted.

Dear Lord, make me loyal in attendance at public worship and faithful in secret prayer that Thy spirit may emanate from me, and that today, in the worship of the sanctuary, I may make it easier for others to pray, easier for others to believe in God and to find Him, easier for troubled minds to find peace and the heavy laden rest.

Teach me during worship to give, as well as to receive, to look for Thee, and to silence the voice of criticism, to travel up some path of thought to reach Thy mind, or some avenue of beauty to reach Thy heart, or some road of challenge to learn Thy will. Help me to respond with all my being, and to seek not only comfort and strength for myself and for others, but to give something to Thee; my worship, my adoration, my love. I adore Thee. I praise Thee for what Thou art. I worship Thee with all my powers. Lord, turn me not away, but accept my poor gifts and use them for Thy glory. I here and now dedicate my life to Thee. For Jesus Christ's sake. Amen.